The Gospel According to Jesus

THE GOSPEL
ACCORDING
TO JESUS

A New Translation and Guide

To His Essential Teachings

For Believers and Unbelievers

STEPHEN MITCHELL

HarperPerennial
A Division of HarperCollinsPublishers

A hardcover edition of this book was published in 1991 by HarperCollins Publishers.

THE GOSPEL ACCORDING TO JESUS. Copyright © 1991 by Stephen Mitchell. All rights reserved. Printed in the United States of America. No part of this book may be used or reproduced in any manner whatsoever without written permission except in the case of brief quotations embodied in critical articles and reviews. For information address HarperCollins Publishers, Inc., 10 East 53rd Street, New York, NY 10022.

HarperCollins books may be purchased for educational, business, or sales promotional use. For information please write: Special Markets Department, HarperCollins Publishers, Inc., 10 East 53rd Street, New York, NY 10022.

First HarperPerennial edition published 1993.
This personal edition published 1995.

Designed and produced by David Bullen.

ISBN 0-06-095146-X

95 96 97 98 99 RRD 10 9 8 7 6 5 4 3 2 1

Contents

*The text of this pocket edition includes the
Introduction and Gospel sections from previous
editions; the extensive Commentary, the notes,
and the appendixes have been omitted for
reasons of length.*

INTRODUCTION

One of the icons on the walls of my study is a picture of Thomas Jefferson, an inexpensive reproduction of the portrait by Rembrandt Peale. The great man looks down over my desk, his longish, once-red hair almost completely gray now, a fur collar draped softly around his neck like a sleeping cat, his handsome features poised in an expression of serenity, amusement, and concern. I honor his serenity and understand his concern. And I like to think that his amusement—the hint of a smile, the left eyebrow raised a fraction of an inch—comes from finding himself placed in the company not of politicians but of saints.

For among the other icons on my walls are the beautiful, Jewish, halo-free face of Jesus by Rembrandt from the Gemäldegalerie in Berlin; a portrait of that other greatest of Jewish teachers, Spinoza; a Ming dynasty watercolor of a delighted bird-watching Taoist who could easily be Lao-tzu himself; a photograph, glowing with love, of the modern Indian sage Ramana Maharshi; and underneath it, surrounded by dried rose petals, a small Burmese statue of the Buddha, perched on a three-foot-tall packing crate stenciled with CHUE LUNG SOY SAUCE, 22 LBS.

Because Jefferson was our great champion of religious freedom, he was attacked as a rabid atheist by the bigots of his day. But he was a deeply religious man, and he spent a good deal of time thinking about Jesus of Nazareth. During the evening hours of one winter month late in his first term as president, after the public business had been put to rest, he began to compile a version of the Gospels that would include only what he considered the authentic accounts and sayings of Jesus. These he snipped out of his King James Bible and pasted onto the pages of a blank book, in more-or-less chronological order. He took up the project again in 1816, when he was seventy-three, eight years after the end of his second term, pasting in the Greek text as well, along with Latin and French translations, in parallel columns. The "wee little book," which he entitled *The Life and Morals of Jesus of Nazareth*, remained in his family until 1904, when it was published by order of the Fifty-seventh Congress and a copy given to each member of the House and Senate.

What is wrong with the old Gospels that made Jefferson want to compile a new one? He didn't talk about this in public, but in his private correspondence he was very frank:

> The whole history of these books [the Gospels] is so defective and doubtful that it seems vain to attempt minute enquiry into it: and such tricks have been played with their text, and with the texts of other books relating to them, that we have a right, from that cause, to entertain much doubt what parts of them are genuine. In the New Testament there is internal evidence that parts of it have proceeded from an extraordinary man; and that other parts are of the fabric of very inferior minds. It is as easy to separate those parts, as to pick out diamonds from dunghills.
>
> *To John Adams, January 24, 1814*

> We must reduce our volume to the simple Evangelists; select, even from them, the very words only of Jesus, paring off the amphibologisms into which they have been led by forgetting often, or not understanding, what had fallen from him, by giving their own misconceptions as his dicta, and expressing unintelligibly for others what they had not understood them-

selves. There will be found remaining the most sublime and benevolent code of morals which has ever been offered to man.

To John Adams, October 12, 1813

Jefferson's robust honesty is always a delight, and never more so than in the Adams correspondence. The two venerable ex-presidents, who had been allies during the Revolution, then bitter political enemies, and who were now, in their seventies, reconciled and mellow correspondents, with an interest in philosophy and religion that almost equaled their fascination with politics—what a pleasure it is to overhear them discussing the Gospels sensibly, in terms that would have infuriated the narrow-minded Christians of their day. But Jefferson, too, called himself a Christian. "To the corruptions of Christianity," he wrote, "I am, indeed, opposed; but not to the genuine precepts of Jesus himself. I am a Christian in the only sense in which he wanted anyone to be: sincerely attached to his doctrines, in preference to all others; ascribing to himself every *human* excellence; and believing he never claimed any other." It is precisely because of his love for Jesus that he had such contempt for the "tricks" that were played with the Gospel texts.

"Tricks" may seem like a harsh word to use about some of the Evangelists' methods. But Jefferson was morally shocked to realize that the words of Jesus had been added to, deleted, altered, and otherwise tampered with as the Gospels were put together. He might have been more lenient if he were writing today, not as a member of a tiny clear-sighted minority, but in an age when textual skepticism is, at last, widely recognized as a path to Jesus, even by devout Christians, even by the Catholic church. For all reputable scholars today acknowledge that the official Gospels were compiled, in Greek, many decades after Jesus' death, by men who had never heard his teaching, and that a great deal of what the "Jesus" of the Gospels says originated not in Jesus' own Aramaic words, which have been lost forever, but in the very different teachings of the early church. And if we often can't be certain of what he said, we can be certain of what he didn't say.

In this book I have followed Jefferson's example. I have selected and translated, from Mark, Matthew, Luke, and (very sparingly) from John, only those passages that seem to me authentic accounts and sayings of Jesus. When there are three accounts of the same incident, I have relied primarily on Mark, the oldest and in certain ways the most trustworthy of the three Synoptic Gospels. I have also included all the teachings from Matthew and from Luke that seemed authentic. And I have eliminated every passage and, even within authentic passages, every verse or phrase that seemed like a later theological or polemical or legendary accretion.

Gospel means "good news." While the Gospels according to Mark, Matthew, Luke, and John are to a large extent teachings *about* Jesus, I wanted to compile a Gospel that would be the teaching *of* Jesus: what he proclaimed about the presence of God: good news as old as the universe. I found, as Jefferson did, that when the accretions are recognized and stripped off, Jesus surprisingly, vividly appears in all his radiance. Like the man in Bunyan's riddle, the more we throw away, the more we have. Or the process of selection can be compared to a diamond cutter giving shape to a magnificent rough stone, until its full, intrinsic brilliance is revealed. Jefferson, of course, was working without any of the precision tools of modern scholarship, as if trying to shape a diamond with an axe. But he knew what a diamond looked like.

The scholarship of the past seventy-five years is an indispensable help in distinguishing the authentic Jesus from the inauthentic. No good scholar, for example, would call the Christmas stories anything but legends, or the accounts of Jesus' trial anything but polemical fiction. And even about the sayings of Jesus, scholars show a remarkable degree of consensus.

In selecting passages from the Gospels, I have always taken seriously the strictly scholarly criteria. But there are no scholarly criteria for spiritual value. Ultimately my decisions were based on what Jefferson called "internal evidence": the evidence provided by the words themselves. The authentic passages are marked by "sublime ideas of the Supreme Being, aphorisms and precepts of the purest morality and benevolence . . . , humility, innocence, and simplicity of manners . . . , with an eloquence and persuasiveness which have not been surpassed." As Jesus said, the more we become sons (or daughters) of God, the more we become like God—generous, compassionate, impartial, serene. It is easy to recognize these qualities in the authentic sayings. They are Jesus' signature.

To put it another way: when I use the word *authentic*, I don't mean that a saying or incident can be proved to originate from the historical Jesus of Nazareth. There are no such proofs; there are only probabilities. And any selection is, by its nature, tentative. I may have included passages which, though filled with Jesus' spirit, were actually created by an editor, or I may have excluded passages whose light I haven't been able to see. But much of the internal evidence seems to me beyond doubt. When we read the parables of the Good Samaritan and the Prodigal Son, or the saying about becoming like children if we wish to enter the kingdom of God, or the passages in the Sermon on the Mount that teach us to be like the lilies of the field and to love our enemies, "so that you may be sons of your Father in heaven; for he makes his sun rise on the wicked and on the good, and sends rain to the righteous and to the unrighteous," we know we are in the presence of the truth. If it wasn't Jesus who said these things, it was (as in the old joke about Shakespeare) someone else by the same name. Here, in the essential sayings, we have words coming from the depths of the human heart, spoken from the most intimate experience of God's compassion: words that can shine into a Muslim's or a Buddhist's or a Jew's heart just as powerfully as into a Christian's. Whoever spoke these words was one of the great world teachers, perhaps the greatest poet among them, and a brother to all the awakened ones. The words are as genuine as words can be. They are the touchstone of everything else about Jesus.

For me, then, Jesus' words are authentic when scholarship indicates that they probably or possibly originated from him and when at the same time they speak with the voice that I hear in the essential sayings. This may seem like circular reasoning. But it isn't reasoning at all; it is a mode of listening.

No careful reader of the Gospels can fail to be struck by the difference between the largeheartedness of such passages and the bitter, badgering tone of some of the passages added by the early church. It is not only the polemical element in the Gospels, the belief in devils, the flashy miracles, and the resurrection itself that readers like Jefferson, Tolstoy, and Gandhi have felt are unworthy of Jesus, but most of all, the direct antitheses to the authentic teaching that were put into "Jesus'" mouth, doctrines and attitudes so offensive that they "have caused good men to reject the whole in disgust." Jesus teaches us, in his sayings and by his actions, not to judge (in the sense of not to condemn), but to keep our hearts open to all people; the later "Jesus" is the archetypal judge, who will float down terribly on the clouds for the world's final rewards and condemnations. Jesus cautions against anger and teaches the love of enemies; "Jesus" calls his enemies "children of the Devil" and attacks them with the utmost vituperation and contempt. Jesus talks of God as a loving father, even to the wicked; "Jesus" preaches a god who will cast the disobedient into everlasting flames. Jesus includes all people when he calls God "your Father in heaven"; "Jesus" says "*my* Father in heaven." Jesus teaches that all those who make peace, and all those who love their enemies, are sons of God; "Jesus" refers to himself as "*the* Son of God." Jesus isn't interested in defining who he is (except for one passing reference to himself as a prophet); "Jesus" talks on and on about himself. Jesus teaches God's absolute forgiveness; "Jesus" utters the horrifying statement that "whoever blasphemes against the Holy Spirit never has forgiveness but is guilty of an eternal sin." The epitome of this narrowhearted, sectarian consciousness is a saying which a second-century Christian scribe put into the mouth of the resurrected Savior at the end of Mark: "Whoever believes and is baptized will be saved, but whoever doesn't believe will be damned." No wonder Jefferson said, with barely contained indignation,

Among the sayings and discourses imputed to him by his biographers, I find many passages of fine imagination, correct morality, and of the most lovely benevolence; and others again of so much ignorance, so much absurdity, so much untruth, charlatanism, and imposture, as to pronounce it impossible that such contradictions should have proceeded from the same being.

To William Short, April 13, 1820

Once the sectarian passages are left out, we can recognize that Jesus speaks in harmony with the supreme teachings of all the great religions: the Upanishads, the Tao Te Ching, the Buddhist sutras, the Zen and Sufi and Hasidic Masters. I don't mean that all these teachings say exactly the same thing. There are many different resonances, emphases, skillful means. But when words arise from the deepest kind of spiritual experience, from a heart pure of doctrines and beliefs, they transcend religious boundaries, and can speak to all people, male and female, bond and free, Greek and Jew.

The eighteenth-century Japanese Zen poet Ryōkan, who was a true embodiment of Jesus' advice to become like a child, said it like this:

In all ten directions of the universe,
there is only one truth.
When we see clearly, the great teachings are the
   same.
What can ever be lost? What can be attained?
If we attain something, it was there from the
   beginning of time.
If we lose something, it is hiding somewhere
   near us.
Look: this ball in my pocket:
can you see how priceless it is?

II

What *is* the gospel according to Jesus? Simply this:
that the love we all long for in our innermost heart
is already present, beyond longing. Most of us can
remember a time (it may have been just a moment)
when we felt that everything in the world was
exactly as it should be. Or we can think of a joy (it
happened when we were children, perhaps, or the
first time we fell in love) so vast that it was no longer
inside us, but we were inside it. What we intuited
then, and what we later thought was too good to be
true, isn't an illusion. It is real. It is realer than the
real, more intimate than anything we can see or

touch, "unreachable," as the Upanishads say, "yet nearer than breath, than heartbeat." The more deeply we receive it, the more real it becomes.

Like all the great spiritual Masters, Jesus taught one thing only: presence. Ultimate reality, the luminous, compassionate intelligence of the universe, is not somewhere else, in some heaven light-years away. It didn't manifest itself any more fully to Abraham or Moses than to us, nor will it be any more present to some Messiah at the far end of time. It is always right here, right now. That is what the Bible means when it says that God's true name is *I am.*

There is such a thing as nostalgia for the future. Both Judaism and Christianity ache with it. It is a vision of the Golden Age, the days of perpetual summer in a world of straw-eating lions and roses without thorns, when human life will be foolproof, and fulfilled in an endlessly prolonged finale of delight. I don't mean to make fun of the messianic vision. In many ways it is admirable, and it has inspired political and religious leaders from Isaiah to Martin Luther King, Jr. But it is a kind of benign insanity. And if we take it seriously enough, if we live it twenty-four hours a day, we will spend all our time working in anticipation, and will never enter the Sabbath of the heart. How moving and at the same time how ridiculous is the story of the Hasidic rabbi who, every morning, as soon as he woke up, would rush out his front door to see if the Messiah had arrived. (Another Hasidic story, about a more mature stage of this consciousness, takes place at the Passover seder. The rabbi tells his chief disciple to go outside and see if the Messiah has come. "But Rabbi, if the Messiah came, wouldn't you know it in here?" the disciple says, pointing to his heart. "Ah," says the rabbi, pointing to his own heart, "but in here, the Messiah has already come.") Who among the now-middle-aged doesn't remember the fervor of the Sixties, when young people believed that love could transform the world? "You may say I'm a dreamer," John Lennon sang, "but I'm not the only one." The messianic dream of the future may be humanity's sweetest dream. But it is a dream nevertheless, as long as there is a separation between inside and outside, as long as we don't transform ourselves. And Jesus, like the Buddha, was a man who had awakened from all dreams.

When Jesus talked about the kingdom of God, he was not prophesying about some easy, danger-free perfection that will someday appear. He was talking about a state of being, a way of living at ease among the joys and sorrows of *our* world. It is possible, he said, to be as simple and beautiful as the birds of the sky or the lilies of the field, who are always within the eternal Now. This state of being is not something alien or mystical. We don't need to earn it. It is already ours. Most of us lose it as we grow up and become self-conscious, but it doesn't disappear forever; it is always there to be reclaimed, though we have to search hard in order to find it. The rich especially have a hard time reentering this state of being; they are so possessed by their possessions, so entrenched in their social power, that it is almost impossible for them to let go. Not that it is easy for any of us. But if we need reminding, we can always sit at the feet of our young children. They, because they haven't yet developed a firm sense of past and future, accept the infinite abundance of the present with all their hearts, in complete trust. Entering the kingdom of God means feeling, as if we were floating in the womb of the universe, that we are being taken care of, always, at every moment.

All spiritual Masters, in all the great religious traditions, have come to experience the present as the only reality. The Gospel passages in which "Jesus" speaks of a kingdom of God in the future can't be authentic, unless Jesus was a split personal-

ity, and could turn on and off two different con-
sciousnesses as if they were hot- and cold-water
faucets. And it is easy to understand how these passages would have been inserted into the Gospel by
disciples, or disciples of disciples, who hadn't understood his teaching. Passages about the kingdom of
God as coming in the future are a dime a dozen in
the prophets, in the Jewish apocalyptic writings of
the first centuries B.C.E., in Paul and the early
church. They are filled with passionate hope, with a
desire for universal justice, and also, as Nietzsche
so correctly insisted, with a festering resentment
against "them" (the powerful, the ungodly). But
they arise from ideas, not from an experience of the
state of being that Jesus called the kingdom of God.

The Jewish Bible doesn't talk much about this
state; it is more interested in what Moses said at the
bottom of the mountain than in what he saw at the
top. But there are exceptions. The most dramatic
is the Voice from the Whirlwind in the Book of
Job, which I have examined at length elsewhere.
Another famous passage occurs at the beginning of
Genesis: God completes the work of creation by
entering the Sabbath mind, the mind of absolute,
joyous serenity; contemplates the whole universe
and says, "Behold, it is very good."

The kingdom of God is not something that will happen, because it isn't something that *can* happen. It can't appear in a world or a nation; it is a condition that has no plural, but only infinite singulars. Jesus spoke of people "entering" it, said that children were already inside it, told one particularly ardent scribe that he, the scribe, was not "far from" it. If only we stop looking forward and backward, he said, we will be able to devote ourselves to seeking the kingdom of God, which is right beneath our feet, right under our noses; and when we find it, food, clothing, and other necessities are given to us as well, as they are to the birds and the lilies. Where else but here and now can we find the grace-bestowing, inexhaustible presence of God? In its light, all our hopes and fears flitter away like ghosts. It is like a treasure buried in a field; it is like a pearl of great price; it is like coming home. When we find it, we find ourselves, rich beyond all dreams, and we realize that we can afford to lose everything else in the world, even (if we must) someone we love more dearly than life itself.

The portrait of Jesus that emerges from the authentic passages in the Gospels is of a man who has emptied himself of desires, doctrines, rules— all the mental claptrap and spiritual baggage that separate us from true life — and has been filled with the vivid reality of the Unnamable. Because he has let go of the merely personal, he is no one, he is everyone. Because he allows God *through* the personal, his personality is like a magnetic field. Those who are drawn to him have a hunger for the real; the closer they approach, the more they can feel the purity of his heart.

What is purity of heart? If we compare God to sunlight, we can say that the heart is like a window. Cravings, aversions, fixed judgments, concepts, beliefs — all forms of selfishness or self-protection — are, when we cling to them, like dirt on the windowpane. The thicker the dirt, the more opaque the window. When there is no dirt, the window is by its own nature perfectly transparent, and the light can stream through it without hindrance.

Or we can compare a pure heart to a spacious, light-filled room. People or possibilities open the door and walk in; the room will receive them, however many they are, for as long as they want to stay, and will let them leave when they want to. Whereas a corrupted heart is like a room cluttered with valuable possessions, in which the owner sits behind a locked door, with a loaded gun.

One last comparison, from the viewpoint of

spiritual practice. To grow in purity of heart is to grow like a tree. The tree doesn't try to wrench its roots out of the earth and plant itself in the sky, nor does it reach its leaves downward into the dirt. It needs both ground and sunlight, and knows the direction of each. Only because it digs into the dark earth with its roots is it able to hold its leaves out to receive the sunlight.

For every teacher who lives in this way, the word of God has become flesh, and there is no longer a separation between body and spirit. Everything he or she does proclaims the kingdom of God. (A visitor once said of the eighteenth-century Hasidic rabbi Dov Baer, "I didn't travel to Mezritch to hear him teach, but to watch him tie his shoelaces.")

People can feel Jesus' radiance whether or not he is teaching or healing; they can feel it in proportion to their own openness. There is a deep sense of peace in his presence, and a sense of respect for him that far exceeds what they have felt for any other human being. Even his silence is eloquent. He is immediately recognizable by the quality of his aliveness, by his disinterestedness and compassion. He is like a mirror for us all, showing us who we essentially are.

The image of the Master:
one glimpse
and we are in love.

Zen Master Ikkyu

He enjoys eating and drinking, he likes to be around women and children; he laughs easily, and his wit can cut like a surgeon's scalpel. His trust in God is as natural as breathing, and in God's presence he is himself fully present. In his bearing, in his very language, he reflects God's deep love for everything that is earthly: for the sick and the despised, the morally admirable and the morally repugnant, for weeds as well as flowers, lions as well as lambs. He teaches that just as the sun gives light to both wicked and good, and the rain brings nourishment to both righteous and unrighteous, God's compassion embraces all people. There are no pre-conditions for it, nothing we need to do first, nothing we have to believe. When we are ready to receive it, it is there. And the more we live in its presence, the more effortlessly it flows through us, until we find that we no longer need external rules or Bibles or Messiahs.

For this teaching which I give you today is not hidden from you, and is not far away. It is not in heaven, for you to say, "Who will go up to heaven and bring it down for us, so that we can hear it and do it?" Nor is it beyond the sea, for you to say, "Who will cross the sea and bring it back for us, so that we can hear it and do it?" But the teaching is very near you: it is in your mouth and in your heart, so that you can do it.

Deuteronomy 30:11ff.

He wants to tell everyone about the great freedom: how it feels when we continually surrender to the moment and allow our hearts to become pure, not clinging to past or future, not judging or being judged. In each person he meets he can see the image of God in which they were created. They are all perfect, when he looks at them from the Sabbath mind. From another, complementary, viewpoint, they are all imperfect, even the most righteous of them, even he himself, because nothing is perfect but the One. He understands that being human *means* making mistakes. When we acknowledge this in all humility, without wanting anything else, we can forgive ourselves, and we can begin correcting our mistakes. And once we forgive ourselves, we can forgive anyone.

He has no ideas to teach, only presence. He has

no doctrines to give, only the gift of his own freedom.

> Tolerant like the sky,
> all-pervading like sunlight,
> firm like a mountain,
> supple like a branch in the wind,
> he has no destination in view
> and makes use of anything
> life happens to bring his way.
>
> Nothing is impossible for him.
> Because he has let go,
> he can care for the people's welfare
> as a mother cares for her child.
>
> *Tao Te Ching, 59*

III

Jesus left us the essence of himself in his teachings, which are all we need to know about him.

We want to know much more, of course. What did he look like? What color were his eyes? Was he tall or short? What did his voice sound like, as he spoke the Aramaic words that were perhaps written down but never preserved? What were the details of the spiritual rebirth that transformed him from a village carpenter into the being whose portrait is in those words? Was he a disciple of John the Baptist? Who were his friends, and what did they talk about after dinner or as they walked through the Galilean countryside? How skillful a teacher was he in his intimate relationships with his disciples? What really happened between Judas and him? Was he married? Was he ever in love? Did he have any premonition that his end would come at such a heartbreakingly early age, and with such great physical agony?

We know so little about his life. A very few facts, and no more. He was baptized by John the Baptist. He taught. He healed. He was crucified by the Romans. The rest is silence, probabilities, and hints. But anyone who can distinguish between the language of legend and the language of human experience knows that his life must have had a very different shape from the one into which it was molded by the piety of the early church.

This is an important matter not only for Jews, agnostics, Buddhists, and others who find their hearts touched by the authentic words of Jesus, but also for Christians. "Is it not time," Emerson asked, "to present this matter of Christianity exactly as it is, to take away all false reverence for Jesus, and not mistake the stream for the source?" We can't begin to see who Jesus was until we remove the layers of interpretation which the centuries have interposed between us and him, and which obscure his true face, like coat after coat of lacquer upon the vibrant colors of a masterpiece.

I understand how difficult even the thought of this may be for some Christians. It is always difficult to let go of our pieties, those small, familiar, comfortable alcoves which we enter when we need to be consoled or reassured that the world is safe. Of course, it is possible to be a traditional Christian, just as in first-century Palestine it was possible to be a scribe or a Pharisee, and live an entirely honorable, even a holy, life. But if we want to go further and enter the kingdom of God, we can't care about safety, or hold on to our beliefs. When the merchant found the pearl of great price, he went and sold everything he had in order to buy it.

We should set aside, first, the Christmas legend. We don't have to eliminate it; it is beautiful and has its place; but we should realize that it is a fairy tale and, though it is suffused with the joyful spirit of Jesus, tells us nothing about his actual birth. Next, all concepts about Jesus, and all his traditional titles

(Messiah, Savior, Redeemer, Son of Man, Son of God), which originated not in his own teaching but in the church's thoughts about him. Then, most of the stories about plots and opposition from Pharisees and others, because they are so deeply tainted by the Evangelists' anti-Semitism, which developed in the decades after Jesus' death, out of the growing mutual hostility between church and synagogue. And finally, the legends of the resurrection, those poignant whistlings in the dark, in which Jesus appears as an insubstantial ghost of himself. "If Christ was not raised," Paul said, "your faith is empty." But faith is larger than any *if*s; and when we trust God completely, we can trust death as well.

So. He was baptized. He taught. He healed. He was crucified by the Romans. What more can we intuit once the legends have been peeled away?

The focal point of a great spiritual Master, the point from which his teachings begin, tells us something important about him. Lao-tzu, like his fraternal twin Spinoza, begins with the vision of wholeness, the current of perfection that flows through all things, the God beyond God. The Buddha begins with the mind; he shows us, with infinite compassion, how to see through our neuroses, into the face we had before our parents were born. Jesus begins with the kingdom of God in the heart. His teachings have such a deep moral resonance that they take us beyond the realm of the moral and make righteousness seem like the most beautiful thing on earth. In this he is prototypically Jewish. What is required of us is to do justly, to love mercy, and to walk humbly with our God. Not "behind": "with."

But few people are ready to enter the kingdom of God. So Jesus has a second focal point: forgiveness. If Lao-tzu's teaching is a circle, Jesus' is an ellipse.

People who are familiar only with Christianity among the great world religions don't realize how surprising this emphasis is. Other great Masters teach forgiveness, to be sure. But for them it is a secondary matter. When we center ourselves in the Tao, surrendering our own will to the will of God-or-Nature, when we purify our mind of the desires and aversions that arise from primal ignorance, then eventually, without any intention or effort on our part, we become the kind of person who finds it easy to forgive personal wrongs.

When you realize where you come from,
you naturally become tolerant,

> disinterested, amused,
> kindhearted as a grandmother,
> dignified as a king.
>
> *Tao Te Ching, 16*

Why did Jesus place such emphasis on forgiveness? Perhaps partly because he felt that this was the most important lesson the people of his time and place needed to learn. But I think there was another reason. An insightful psychotherapist will notice that many of her patients are confronting, at a more acute stage, issues that she is currently confronting in herself. They are drawn to her as to a relatively clear mirror, and the mirroring is mutual: in them too she can see herself. Even a great Master teaches what he needs, or once needed, to learn.

The emotion that informs Jesus' teaching about forgiveness is so intense, so filled with the exhilaration of forgiving and being forgiven, that it must have come from a profound personal experience. I would like to feel my way into this experience by examining some hints that the Gospels give about his position in the original holy trinity: the father, the son, and the mother.

IV

The first thing we ought to realize about Jesus'
life is that he grew up as an illegitimate child. On
this point both traditional Christians and non-
Christians can fully agree, because even those who
believe in the virginal conception don't believe that
the angel Gabriel appeared to everyone else in Nazareth, to assure them that Mary's child had been
fathered by God.

We say that she was highly honored among
women. . . . It is true that Mary conceived the
child in a miraculous fashion, but she nevertheless did it "after the manner of women" [Gene-
sis 18:11], and pregnancy is a time of anxiety,
distress, and paradox. It is true that the angel
was a ministering spirit, but he wasn't a med-
dler: he didn't appear to the other girls in Israel
and say, "Don't despise Mary; the extraordinary
is happening to her." The angel appeared only
to Mary, and no one could understand her. Has
any woman been as humiliated as Mary was, and
isn't it true here also that the one whom God
blesses he curses in the same breath? This is the

spirit's view of Mary, and she is not—it is revolting that I have to say this, but it is even more
revolting that people have inanely and sancti-
moniously depicted her in this way—she is not
a lady lounging in her gorgeous robes and play-
ing with an infant god.

Søren Kierkegaard, *Fear and Trembling*

If an angel appeared, he appeared only to Mary,
and she was unmarried, and her too-early pregnancy
was a scandal to the whole village. There would
have been no corroboration of the miracle, no protection. She would have been exposed to the contempt of her neighbors not only for the six months
after her swollen belly became visible, but would
have had to eat derision and insult with her daily
bread for as long as she lived. As for the social effects
on a young child: growing up with the shame of
being called a bastard must be almost as painful as
being illegitimate in fact.

But let us suppose that Jesus was conceived and
born in the ordinarily miraculous way:

I, too, am mortal, like every human,
Descended from the first man formed of the
    dust.

I was molded into flesh in a mother's womb;
For nine months I was compacted in blood
From the semen of a man and sexual pleasure.
I, too, breathed-in the common air,
Was laid on the earth that bears us all,
And my first sound was a wail, like everyone
    else.
No king is born differently; for there is just
One way into life, and one way out.

Wisdom of Solomon 7:1-6

For most people, and for Christians who don't accept the virginal conception literally but see it as a pious legend and a metaphor, the evidence of Jesus' illegitimacy is fairly clear. There are four passages in the official Gospels, and one in the Gospel of Thomas, that hint at it. (Of course, we have to read between the lines to realize their meaning; where the Evangelists want us to read black, we must read white.) This matter has been studied in great detail by contemporary scholars; the most exhaustive treatment is *The Illegitimacy of Jesus* by Jane Schaberg. I will just quote the five passages, with a few comments.

1. From the infancy narrative in Matthew:

Now the birth of Jesus happened in this way.
Mary, his mother, was engaged to Joseph, but
before they came together to live, she was found
to be pregnant by the Holy Spirit. And Joseph,
being a just man and not wanting to put her to
public shame, decided to divorce her quietly.
But as he was considering this, behold, an angel
of the Lord appeared to him in a dream, and
said to him, "Joseph, son of David, do not be
afraid to take Mary as your wife, for what has
been begotten in her is of the Holy Spirit. And
she will give birth to a son, and you shall name
him Jesus."

Behind the author's (and the angel's) explanation
that Mary was made pregnant by the Holy Spirit is
an accusation that must have been current during
Jesus' lifetime. As the Catholic scholar Raymond E.
Brown writes:

Matthew tells us of the rumor that Mary's pregnancy was adulterous. The explanation given by
the angel may have set Joseph's mind at ease; but
in the implicit logic of Matthew's account there
would have been no way to disguise the fact that

Jesus would be born indecently early after Mary was taken to Joseph's home. Obviously, Matthew is facing a story that is in circulation, and factual data that he cannot deny: he does not and seemingly cannot reply that Jesus was born at the proper interval after Joseph and Mary came to live together. Traces of the rumor of irregularity of birth and illegitimacy appear elsewhere in the New Testament.... Since it is not easy to dismiss such a persistent charge, which may be as old as Christianity itself, those [Christians] who deny the virginal conception cannot escape the task of explaining how the rumor of illegitimacy and irregularity of birth arose and how they would answer it without accepting a very unpleasant [sic] alternative.

2. From the genealogy at the beginning of Matthew's Gospel:

Abraham begat Isaac, Isaac begat Jacob, Jacob begat Judah and his brothers, Judah begat Perez and Zarah out of Tamar, Perez begat Hezron, Hezron begat Ram, Ram begat Aminadab, Aminadab begat Nahshon, Nahshon begat Salmon, Salmon begat Boaz out of Rahab, Boaz begat

Obed out of Ruth, Obed begat Jesse, Jesse begat King David, David begat Solomon out of Uriah's wife, . . .

The peculiar feature in this list is the mention of the four women (in the divergent genealogy in Luke 3:23ff., no women are mentioned). Morton Smith explains the significance of their presence here:

Matthew's genealogy of Jesus (1:2-16) refers to only four women besides Mary: they are Tamar, whose children were born of incest; Rahab, the madam of a brothel; Ruth, a non-Israelite, who got her second husband by solicitation, if not fornication, and so became the great-grand-mother of David (Ruth 4:21f.); and Bathsheba ("the wife of Uriah"), whose relations with David began in adultery, though she became the mother of Solomon. That the author of a genealogy for a Messiah should have chosen to mention only these four women requires an explanation. The most likely one is that Matthew wanted to excuse Mary by these implied analogies.

3. From Mark's account of Jesus' failure at Nazareth:

> And when the Sabbath came, he began to teach in the synagogue, and many people who heard him were bewildered, and said, "Where does this fellow get such stuff?" and "What makes *him* so wise?" and "How can he be a miracle-worker? Isn't this the carpenter, the son of Mary, the brother of James and Joseph and Judas and Simon, and aren't his sisters here with us?" And they were prevented from believing in him.

In English, "the son of Mary" gives no idea of the phrase's connotation in Aramaic or Hebrew. In Semitic usage, a man was normally called "[name] son of [father's name]"; if he was called "[name] son of [mother's name]," it indicated that his father was unknown and that he was illegitimate. According to a later Jewish legal principle, "A man is illegitimate when he is called by his mother's name, for a bastard has no father." That is why in my version of the Gospel I have translated *ho huios tēs Marias*— "the son of Mary"—as "Mary's bastard" (it is impossible to know exactly how crude an insult the Aramaic would have been).

4. In the Gospel of John we find the following debate between "Jesus" and "the Jews":

["Jesus" says:] "I know that you are Abraham's descendants, but you are trying to kill me, because my teaching has found no place in you. What I have seen with the Father, I speak; what you have heard from the father, you do."

They answered, "Our father is Abraham."

Jesus said to them, "If you are children of Abraham, do the works of Abraham. But now you are trying to kill me, a man who has spoken the truth to you, which I heard from God. Abraham did not do that. You are doing the works of your father."

They said to him, "*We* were not born of fornication. We have one father: God."

Jesus said to them, "If God were your father, you would love me.... Your father is the devil, and you want to do your father's will. He was a murderer from the beginning...."

John is almost never a trustworthy witness to the historical Jesus, but in this accusation, as Jane Schaberg explains, he seems to have preserved an authentic strand of tradition. ("Jesus'" answer, in its hatred and demonization of the Jews, is, of course, anything but authentic.)

In the midst of this argument, the opponents say, "*We* were not born of fornication" (*Hymeis ek porneias ou gegennēmetha*), the emphasis on "we" implying "but you were," that is, implying that Jesus was illegitimate. The Jews meet Jesus' challenge to their religious or spiritual legitimacy by a challenge to his physical legitimacy. The suggestion of Jesus' illegitimacy here is subtle and is drawn from pre-gospel tradition.

5. Finally, there is a spine-tingling verse from the Gospel of Thomas: "He who knows his [true] Father [i.e., God] and Mother [i.e., the Holy Spirit] will be called the son of a whore." In this verse, which I think originates from Jesus (though it is tinged with Gnostic theology), we can hear the taunts and insults of the Nazareth villagers echoing down through the centuries.

If someone wished to choose the most difficult starting point for a human life, short of being born diseased or deformed, he might well choose to be born illegitimate. In the ancient world, both Jewish and Roman, illegitimacy was considered one of the most shameful of human conditions. The central biblical text is Deuteronomy 23:3: "No *mamzer* shall enter the assembly of YHVH, even to the tenth generation" (*mamzer* is usually translated as "bastard," and interpreted as "the child of an adulterous union").

The *mamzerim* were forbidden marriage with the priestly families, Levites, legitimate Israelites, and even with illegitimate descendants of priests. At the end of the first century C.E. their rights to inherit from their natural fathers were in dispute. They could not hold public office, and if they took part in a court decision, the decision was invalidated. Their families' share in Israel's final redemption was vigorously argued. The word *mamzer* was considered one of the worst insults to a man. *Mamzerim* were among those called the "excrement of the community."

This was by no means only a Jewish attitude; the contempt for illegitimate children was just as strong among Gentiles. We can see it clearly in the polemical treatise *Contra Celsum*, which the Christian theologian Origen wrote, in about the year 248, to refute the various refutations of Christianity put forth by the philosopher Celsus. In the following passage, Origen is responding to Celsus's accusation that Jesus was born illegitimate. I will quote this at some length, because it gives us an insight into the minds of the men who created Christian doctrine:

> It was inevitable that those who did not accept the miraculous birth of Jesus would have invented some lie. But the fact that they did not do this convincingly, but kept as part of the story that the virgin did not conceive Jesus by Joseph, makes the lie obvious to people who can see through fictitious stories and show them up. Is it reasonable that a man who ventured to do such great things for mankind in order that, so far as in him lay, all Greeks and barbarians in expectation of the divine judgment might turn from evil and act in every respect acceptably to the Creator of the universe, should have had, not a miraculous birth, but a birth more illegitimate and disgraceful than any? As addressing Greeks, and Celsus in particular who, whether he holds Plato's doctrines or not, nevertheless quotes them, I would ask this question. Would He who sends souls down into human bodies compel a man to undergo a birth more shameful than any, and not even have brought him into human life by legitimate marriage, when he was to do such

great deeds and to teach so many people and to convert many from the flood of evil? Or is it more reasonable (and I say this now following Pythagoras, Plato, and Empedocles, whom Celsus often mentions) that there are certain secret principles by which each soul that enters a body does so in accordance with its merits and former character? It is therefore probable that this soul, which lived a more useful life on earth than many men (to avoid appearing to beg the question by saying "all" men), needed a body which was not only distinguished among human bodies, but was also superior to all others....

Suppose that all bodies conform to the habits of their souls; then for the soul that was to live a miraculous life on earth and to do great things, a body was necessary, not, as Celsus thinks, produced by the adultery of Panthera [a Roman soldier who was rumored to be Jesus' real father] and a virgin (for the offspring of such impure intercourse must rather have been some stupid man who would harm men by teaching licentiousness, unrighteousness, and other evils, and not a teacher of self-control, righteousness, and the other virtues), but, as the prophets foretold, the offspring of a virgin, who according to the promised sign should give birth to a child whose name was significant of his work, showing that at his birth God would be with men.

For people living in the first century, then, whether they were Jews, pagans, or Christians, it was inconceivable that an illegitimate child could grow up to be a decent man, much less a prophet or a great spiritual teacher. They didn't have a category for that. Most people still don't. Nor do they understand what Jesus meant when he said, "Nothing can defile a man from the outside; it is only what comes out of a man that defiles him."

I don't think that we can fully appreciate who Jesus became unless we realize the overwhelming difficulties he must have had as an illegitimate child in a small provincial town, which one has to assume was fairly harsh and moralistic when it dealt with such matters. Mary may have been the most loving of mothers, and Jesus himself was no doubt an unusually gifted and joyful child; but even so, the atmosphere of public contempt and derision must have felt like a continual attack on his soul. When we imagine such a beginning, our admiration for him can only increase. Conventional piety, of course, would like to urge us, as it compelled Matthew and Luke, to give the infant Jesus the accoutrements of holiness that we see in all the paintings: angels, auras, sumptuous gifts, visiting dignitaries who worship him on bended knees. But there is a deeper piety of the actual. And that deeper piety shows us that God is to be found not in the *should be*, but in the *is*.

It is remarkable what an opposite and complementary shape the life of the Buddha had. He was born the son of a king, and in order to become himself, he had to overcome the difficulties that arise from being rich, all the temptations of luxury and power, the camel-and-the-eye-of-the-needle syndrome. We can see the respective beginnings of these two great men as opposite ends of the spectrum that is the human condition. Together, their meaning is that no life is so sheltered or so shamed that it can't be transformed into a vehicle of God's grace, a vessel filled with the deepest charity and wisdom. So capable are we of using whatever materials we are given; so irresistible is the phototropism of the human soul.

Even for Christians, I think, even theologically, it is appropriate for Jesus to have taken on the difficult karma of opprobrium, as Blake taught in his wonderfully perceptive late poem "The Everlasting Gospel":

> Was Jesus born of a virgin pure
> With narrow soul and looks demure?
> If he intended to take on sin
> The mother should an harlot been.
> ....
> Or what was it which he took on
> That he might bring salvation:
> A body subject to be tempted,
> From neither pain nor grief exempted,
> Or such a body as might not feel
> The passions that with sinners deal?

What more powerful way could there have been for Jesus to become one with all the outcasts and despised of the earth than to be born illegitimate? Taking on this particular incarnation would mean experiencing, in his own body, at the most vulnerable time of a human life, the most intense shame, wretchedness, and separation, so that he could eventually include and invite everyone into the kingdom of God. Rather than the famous misinterpreted verse from First Isaiah about a "virgin" giving birth to a son, Second Isaiah's description of the despised figure known as the Suffering Servant seems truly prophetic of Jesus.

> He is despised and rejected of men; a man of sorrows, and acquainted with grief: and we hid as it were our faces from him; he was despised, and we esteemed him not. Surely he hath borne our griefs, and carried our sorrows: yet we did esteem him stricken, smitten of God, and afflicted.

Prophetic not of his death, but of his birth.

V

Only one word has come down to us directly from the lips of Jesus in its original Aramaic: *abba*, "father." Mark quotes it in the context of the prayer at Gethsemane, which may or may not be historical; but it is certain that Jesus used the word often, and that it lies behind the *our father*'s and the *your father*'s of the authentic sayings. And while his teaching about the presence, here, now, of the kingdom of God is so simple that it may seem absurd to some and immoral to others—a stumbling block to the Jews and to the Greeks foolishness—his description of God as an infinitely loving father is a teaching everybody can understand.

Few of us, though, can feel the intensity of what Jesus meant when he said *abba*. Actually, we don't have a word for it. Our word *father* reflects a personal and social reality which is a much diluted version of the reality a first-century Jewish father had for his children: a position of absolute power, for both good and evil, which commanded a fear or a respect that we can barely conceive of. To really translate the word, we would have to translate the culture.

For Jesus, the Father is pure generosity, pure creativity, the embodiment of the first hexagram of the I Ching, the archetypal power that generates the whole universe, that blesses and keeps and makes its face shine upon all its children and gives them peace. And not only absolute creative power, but also absolute mercy, a quality we associate more with mothers. The prophets, in fact, speak of God as feeling a kind of motherly love for Israel, since the Hebrew verb *rhm*, usually translated as "to have mercy or compassion," derives from a root that means "womb."

The Psalms and the prophets occasionally speak of God as a father, even as a mother. But the image is not a common one in the Bible. It became much more common in later Judaism; as the Aramaic scholar Gustaf Dalman said, "Jesus adopted this term for God from the popular usage of his time." Of Dalman's many examples, I will cite two. The first is from the Book of Jubilees:

> "Their [the Israelites'] souls will attach themselves to Me and to all My commandments, and My commandments will return to them; and I will be to them a father, and they will be My children. And they will all be called children of the living God; and every angel and every spirit will surely recognize that these are My children, and that I am their father in sincerity and righteousness, and that I love them."

The second is from the second-century rabbi Yehuda ben Tema:

> Be bold as a leopard, quick as an eagle, swift as a gazelle, and strong as a lion to do the will of your heavenly Father.

So Jesus' teaching was not original, in the strict sense of the word. The subject of originality is a sore point with certain kinds of literal-minded Christian and Jewish scholars. The former try to

prove that Jesus was, the latter that he wasn't, original; and the opposing idea, that he wasn't, or was,
makes these scholars feel as squirmy as someone
who has sat on an anthill at a picnic. They are looking in the wrong direction. Originality has nothing
to do with priority. An image is like a musical key;
just because someone used G-minor before doesn't
make Mozart a copycat. When the Holy Spirit
comes, all things are made new. Jesus wasn't the
first to speak of God as a loving father, or even to
say "Be like your Father." But his sayings, in their
intimacy and passion, speak from the most profound experience of God's fatherness, and express
the intimacy and passion with which he lived it.

VI

To appreciate Jesus' teaching about God as an infinitely loving father, we don't *have* to relate it to
Jesus' life. But I think that the teaching gains in
richness and poignancy when we do.

If there is one reality that marks what we might
call the emotional life of Jesus, as glimpsed through
his various sayings, it is the presence of the divine
father and the absence of a human father. This is
entirely in keeping with the probability that he

grew up as an illegitimate child. We don't know if Mary ever married, though presumably she did, since she had four other sons and at least two daughters. The father, or stepfather, is never mentioned in the authentic verses of the Gospels. (References to Joseph occur only in Matthew's and Luke's infancy legends.) According to a later verse in Matthew, Jesus once said, "Don't call any man on earth 'father,' for you have just one father, and he is in heaven."

Every illegitimate child must feel intense longing for a father: not only the longing that orphans feel, for an adult male presence at the core of their life, but also for legitimation, for a father—for *the* father—to come and say, "Yes, you do belong to the human community. You are of infinite value, like every human being. You are my beloved child."

We know nothing about Jesus' enlightenment experience, which changed him from carpenter to Master, from "son of a whore" to a son of God. (We know nothing . . . we know nothing. . . . Even when I don't say it explicitly, this phrase will be a kind of silent ground bass that accompanies everything I try to intuit about Jesus' life.) The experience may have happened at any time: as he was hammering nails in his workshop, as he was walking on the pebbly shore of the Sea of Galilee, perhaps as he was fasting and meditating in the wilderness. The Gospel of Mark implies that it happened while he was being baptized by John the Baptist, and that may be the historical reality. Before I try to imagine the event more fully, I need to talk about the way it is used by the four Evangelists.

It is the first event that we know of in Jesus' life, and along with his crucifixion by the Romans, it is, as I said before, one of our very few historical certainties. But we have only the most meager information about it: "At that time Jesus came from Nazareth in Galilee, and was baptized in the Jordan by John." Just that sentence. We don't know what brought Jesus to be baptized or what kind of experience it was. The heavenly voice and the descent of the Holy Spirit in the form of a dove are explanations added by the early church. But it is possible that the mythological form both obscures and preserves something of the actual experience.

In almost all the ancient manuscripts of Mark and Luke, the heavenly voice says, "You are my beloved son; with you I am well pleased" (Matthew recasts the sentence in the third person). But at Luke 3:22, a few ancient manuscripts read, "You are my son; this day I have begotten you." This is a quotation from Psalm 2; since the verse is also quoted in Acts and Hebrews, it must have been current in the early church. Again, there is no way to know if this account is just Christology or if it actually contains some memory of Jesus talking about the event, telling about how he felt reborn, begotten by God, in and through this experience.

It is obvious that the Gospel writers felt uncomfortable with the fact of the baptism. One reason is Jesus' subordination to John the Baptist. How could the Messiah have bowed before the Messenger?

We know that during Jesus' life and in the early years after his death, there was intense competition between his disciples and the disciples of John. Luke says that Apollos, who later became an apostle, at first "understood only the baptism of John," implying that it was inferior to the Christian baptism. Similarly, according to Luke, when Paul arrived in Ephesus, he asked the congregation,

> "Did you receive the Holy Spirit when you became believers?"
>
> And they said, "No, we didn't even hear that there is a Holy Spirit."

And he said, "Then what were you baptized into?"

And they said, "Into John's baptism."

And Paul said, "John baptized with a baptism of repentance, and he told the people to believe in the one who was to come after him, that is, in Jesus."

And when they heard this, they were baptized into the name of the Lord Jesus.

(Since no texts from the Baptist's disciples have come down to us, we don't know what they thought of Jesus. They may not have thought of him at all. But if they did, given the ego investment that disciples have in the superiority of their teacher, it is likely that they put him in, at best, second place.)

So Jesus' baptism would have been an acute problem, except for a relatively mature disciple. To guard against the conclusion that John was somehow superior to Jesus, Mark puts these words into the Baptist's mouth: "One who is stronger than I is coming after me, and I am not worthy to stoop down and untie the thong of his sandals. I have baptized you with water, but he will baptize you with the Holy Spirit." Matthew adds a conversation in which John himself asks the troubling question about the baptism and confesses his inferiority directly to Jesus:

> Then Jesus came from Galilee to the Jordan to be baptized by John. John, trying to prevent him, said, "Why are you coming to me? *I* need to be baptized by *you*!" But Jesus answered him, "Let it happen now; for it is proper that we fulfill all righteousness in this way." Then he let it happen.

Luke solves the problem by putting John in prison and having Jesus baptized in the passive voice, by an undesignated agent:

> When all the people were being baptized, and when Jesus too had been baptized and was praying, the heavens opened. . . .

The Fourth Gospel never mentions that Jesus was baptized, and has John recognize him as the Son of God the moment he sees him.

The point of all this editorial activity is to explain an event which, according to the writers' beliefs, should not have taken place. The event is incontrovertible precisely because of their embarrassment. No writer would have invented a detail that was so troubling.

But there is an even more embarrassing aspect to the baptism. As Mark says, "All the people were baptized by [John] in the river Jordan, confessing their sins." If Jesus was "a man without sin," as the later, and probably the early, disciples thought—or even more, if he was the preexistent Son of God— how could he have had any sins to confess, and why did he feel the need for baptism? This question was posed explicitly in the fourth-century *Debates of Archelaus, Bishop of Mesopotamia, and the Heresiarch Mani*:

> *Archelaus:* If Jesus was not baptized, neither is any of us baptized. But if there is no baptism, neither will there be any remission of sins, but everyone will die in his sins.
>
> *Mani:* Therefore is baptism given for the remission of sins?
>
> *Archelaus:* Yes.
>
> *Mani:* But Christ was baptized: Had he therefore sinned?
>
> *Archelaus:* Not so; rather, "He was made sin for us," taking on our sins.

The Evangelists deal with the problem by immediately focusing attention on Jesus' vision (according to Mark, followed by Matthew, only Jesus could see the dove; Luke implies that everyone present could see it; according to John, it was visible only to the Baptist.) The writer of the Gospel of the Nazoreans, which probably dates from the early second century, acknowledges the problem by denying the baptism:

> The mother of the Lord and his brothers said to him, "John the Baptist baptizes for the forgiveness of sins; let us go and be baptized by him."
>
> But Jesus said to them, "What sin have I committed, that I should go and be baptized by him? Unless what I just said is a sin of ignorance."

There is no problem about the baptism unless we hold on to the idea that Jesus is superhuman, an idea that he himself certainly didn't have. "Why do you call me good?" he once said to an earnest inquirer who called him "Good Rabbi"; "no one is good except God alone." It would be a childish view of him to think that he never caused suffering or made mistakes. (The Hebrew word for "sin" means "to miss the mark.") And in his own view of himself, he undoubtedly felt, like anyone who has spent a great amount of time in prayer or meditation, that he was just one partial expression of the divine whole: the moon reflected, however clearly, in a dewdrop. That he felt imperfect and fallible simply means that he was one of us.

If the account of the official Gospels does contain some authentic memory, what can the actual event have been like for Jesus? Here we have to look behind the mythologized language: the sky splitting apart, the Holy Spirit descending as a dove. What we are left with is the voice of God, in one of its myriad forms.

It isn't hard to imagine the external details of the baptism scene: the crowds of enthusiastic devotees, the fiery-eyed Baptist, unkempt, "clothed in camel's hair, with a belt of animal hide around his waist," and preaching with the greatest passion and urgency, the immersions, the cheers, the groans of emotional release, the clumps of friends and relatives who stand together, dripping, on the riverbank. For many of these people the baptism was undoubtedly a profound experience. But Jesus' experience must have been fundamentally different. Repentance can be a transitory emotion, and the revival meeting is notorious for ecstasies that vanish at the threshold of the ego.

I see him as a sincere young man who, on some unconscious level, was still struggling with the pain of his childhood, and who had not yet penetrated to the place of pure light. Perhaps it was the ferocious intensity of John, the first prophet he had ever met, that precipitated the experience. But as Jesus looked into his eyes, or as he was thrust under the surface of the Jordan River, something broke open, not in the heavens but in his own heart. He felt an ecstatic release, a cleansing of those painfully hidden childhood emotions of humiliation and shame, a sense of being taken up, once and for all, into the embrace of God. "You are my beloved son; this day I have begotten you."

The passage which, for me, sheds the most light on what this experience must have felt like is the parable of the Prodigal Son. The story, as Jesus tells it, is beyond praise; in its tenderness and compassion, it speaks to all of us. Its economy and pathos are unsurpassed in the literature of the world, and its artistry is even more apparent to those familiar with the similar parable in the Lotus Sutra of Mahayana Buddhism, which rambles on and on like a well-meaning, dimwitted uncle.

Jesus' parable was primarily intended for the righteous. Its lesson is that those who have always remained with God, as the older son remained with his father, shouldn't feel resentful toward those who have truly repented and returned, but should receive them openheartedly, with joy, as the father received his younger son. That is the ostensible teaching, and it is an extremely important and moving lesson. But most people, when they think of or talk about the parable, remember only its first part. The reason for this, it seems to me, is not only that most people identify themselves with the younger son, but also that the unconscious center of gravity of the parable itself, its most intense emotion, lies in the first part.

It begins with the father and his two sons, but quickly focuses attention on the younger one.

> There once was a man who had two sons. And the younger one said to him, "Father, let me have my share of the estate." So he divided his property between them. And not many days afterward, having turned his share into money, the younger son left and traveled to a distant country, and there he squandered his inheritance in riotous living. And after he had spent it

all, a severe famine arose in that country; and he was destitute. And he went and hired himself out to a citizen of that country, who sent him to his farm to feed the pigs. And he longed to fill his belly with the husks that the pigs were eating; and no one would give him any food.

Later I will examine the story in detail. For now, I want to consider its emotion. Jesus' interest here is not in telling how the younger son arrived at his destitute condition, but in describing that condition. There is an almost unbearable sense of degradation. The son is treated, and feels like, the lowest of the low. He is cut off from all human society, reduced to spending his days taking care of pigs, the unclean animal par excellence, and is too disgusted to eat the carob pods that they feed on in their contented piggish way.

Christian teaching identifies Jesus with the father in the parable. But in a parable, as in a poem or a dream, the teller is *all* the images and characters. And given the focus on the figure of the younger son, given the depth of emotion emanating from him, it is clear that Jesus has particularly, and wholly, entered into *him* at this point. Of course, this identification may be simply a matter of his general empathy with the poor, the bereft, and the downtrodden. But it is hard for me not to think that he has entered so deeply into the younger son because he himself had once felt that way. I am not suggesting that there is a correspondence of details between the story and his life, or that he ever lived prodigally. But any separation from God is painful to a young man of Jesus' gifts, and the smallest mistake appears huge under the microscope of his moral conscience. Not even the greatest Masters were spared the process of spiritual death and rebirth. For Jesus, the rebirth must have been particularly astonishing, because it had to include and overcome the sustained indignities of his childhood. "The way down and the way up are one and the same," as Heraclitus tells us. When we sink to the bottom of our lostness, we can begin to find ourselves.

And when he came to himself, he said, "How many of my father's hired men have more than enough to eat, while I am dying of hunger. I will get up and go to my father, and say to him, 'Father, I have sinned against God and against you, and I am no longer worthy to be called your son. Let me be like one of your hired men.'" And he got up, and went to his father. And while he was still a long way off, his father ̣w him, and was moved with compassion, and ̣o him, and threw his arms around him, and ̣ him. And the son said to him, "Father, I ̣ed against God and against you, and I ̣er worthy to be called your son." But ̣id to his servants, "Quick, bring out t ̣ ̣e we have and put it on him; and put a r ̣ ̣ on his hand, and sandals on his feet. And bring the fatted calf, and kill it; and let us eat and make merry. For this son of mine was dead, and he has come back to life; he was lost, and is found."

Suddenly the younger son comes to himself, becomes himself, in realizing how lost he is, though he is not so lost as to feel that he can't return to his father. No sooner does he realize that he can return, than he *does* return; no sooner does he realize that he is unworthy to be called his father's son, than the father runs to him and embraces him and treats him like the most worthy of sons. "You are my beloved son; this day I have begotten you."

I don't want to suggest that Jesus be identified only with the younger son. It is also true that he is the father, that wonderful figure whose delicate, loving treatment of the older son calls for as much admiration as his unconditional acceptance of the younger son. And he is also the older son, whose grievances are stated harshly but fairly, and whom the parable treats with the tolerance and respect so disastrously lacking in the inauthentic Gospel sayings about the righteous. But if we look for the parable's center of gravity, we can recognize that Jesus is the younger son at least as much as he is the father. And when the son returns to the father, all his shame and sorrow and unworthiness are taken up into the father's uncontainable joy. At this point, the story steps out of the son's consciousness into the father's; in a sense, the son becomes the father. There is no longer any difference between the exhilaration of being forgiven and the joy of forgiving.

One further question about the parable cries out to be asked, and Erik Erikson has asked it acutely:

> Even lengthy parables can be summarized in a brief saying. I think the last dozen words of the Prodigal Son will do: "Your brother was dead, and is alive; he was lost, and is found." Again, then, the Way is "within" and "amidst you." And the Abba was steadfast in loving both these

sons—so different in familial status and in personality. Almost a mother, some readers may be tempted to say, and, indeed, as one reviews this parable's theme of the healing of the generational process, one cannot help asking: was there, in this earthly vision of the comparison, no mother, either dead or alive? And if alive, was she not called to say hello, too?

As in the parable, so in Jesus' life. After he returned to his Father, was there no mother to greet him? I would like to consider this question next.

VII

Jesus gives us a most vivid example of what it feels like to live in the continual presence of love, in the present and only tense of the verb *God*. His teaching is lucid through and through. Or almost through and through. The one point of unclarity is the family; in particular, the mother. I don't mean this as a criticism of him, but as a simple perception. I would like to take a look at this unclarity, which allows us a rare insight into the workshop of his heart. But before I examine the relevant verses, I need to put them in perspective.

We can use different metaphors to describe the experience that changed Jesus. It is the kind of experience that all the great spiritual Masters have had, and want us to have as well. Jesus called this experience "entering the kingdom of God." We can also call it "rebirth" or "enlightenment" or "awakening." The images implicit in these words come from experiences that we all know: the birth of a child, the light of the sun, the passage from sleep to what we ordinarily call consciousness. Any of these images can be helpful in pointing to a realm of being which most people have forgotten. It *is* like being born into true life, or like the sun streaming into a room that has remained dark for a long time, or like waking up from a dream, or, as Jesus must have felt, like returning home to the Father. And each of these images contains a further truth, if we follow it attentively. Being reborn is only the first stage of a new life, and doesn't mean coming into full spiritual maturity: the infant has a lot of growing up to do before it is self-sufficient. Awakening doesn't necessarily mean arriving at full consciousness: the dreams are gone, but we may still be sleepy, and not truly alert. Or, to return to the image of sunlight passing through a window: the area that has been suddenly wiped clean of selfishness and self-protection—desires, fears, rules, concepts—may be the whole windowpane, or it may be a spot the size of a dime. The sunlight that shines through the small transparent spot is the same light that can shine through a whole windowpane, but there is much less of it, and if someone stands with his nose pressed to one of the other, opaque spots, he will hardly see any light at all.

Two examples. First, Paul of Tarsus, the greatest and yet the most misleading of the earliest Christian writers. It is obvious that Paul's experience on the road to Damascus was a genuine and powerful one. Who can deny the sunlight streaming through his famous praise of love in First Corinthians? And there are a number of other passages where his mind and heart are transparent. But Paul came to his experience with a particularly difficult character: arrogant, self-righteous, filled with murderous hatred of his opponents, terrified of God, oppressed by what he felt as the burden of the Law, overwhelmed by his sense of sin. In terms of the metaphor, his windowpane was caked with grime.

There are things I admire about Paul: his courage, his passion, his loving concern for the Gentiles, his great eloquence, the incredible energy with which he whirled around the Mediterranean for, as he thought, the glory of God. But in a spiritual sense, he was very unripe. The narrow-minded, fire-breathing, self-tormenting Saul was still alive and kicking inside him. He didn't understand Jesus at all. He wasn't even *interested* in Jesus; just in his own idea of the Christ. "Even though we once knew Christ according to the flesh," he wrote, "we no longer regard him in this way." In other words, it isn't relevant to know Jesus as a person of flesh and blood or to hear, much less do, what he taught; the only thing necessary for a Christian is to believe that Jesus was the Son of God and that he died in atonement for our sins. Like the writer of Revelation, Paul harbored a great deal of violence in his mind, which he projected onto visions of cosmic warfare, and onto an image of God as a punitive father, and he most ignorantly believed in what Spinoza describes as "a prince, God's enemy, who against God's will entraps and deceives very many men, whom God then hands over to this master of wickedness to be tortured for eternity." After his conversion, there was indeed a transparent area in his mind, but most of the window was still opaque. And since he thought he was in possession of the truth, he made no effort to clean the rest of the window. The experience that should have been just the beginning of his spiritual life became the beginning and the end of it. We can feel in the writings of Paul the Christian some of the same egotism, superstition, and intolerance that marred the character of Saul the Pharisee.

As a second and contrary example, perhaps the greatest example of patience and meticulousness in the history of religion, I would like to propose Chao-chou, who lived during the golden age of Zen in T'ang dynasty China. He experienced enlightenment in 795, when he was seventeen years old, then remained with his teacher for forty years, refining his insight and gradually dissolving his opacities and character flaws. Zen Master Kuei-shan, his contemporary, describes this process:

> Through meditation a student may gain thoughtless thought, become suddenly enlightened, and realize his original nature. But there is still a basic delusion. Therefore he should be taught to eliminate the manifestations of karma, which cause the remaining delusion to rise to the surface. There is no other way of cultivation.

Anyone who has undergone the experience of spiritual transformation knows how agonizing it can be. It is like cleaning the heart with a piece of steel wool. Or like that terrace in Dante's *Purgatorio* where the spirits who have stopped for a while to talk, dive back into the flames. They choose to return to the excruciating pain, to stand again in the pale blue archways of primal grief or rage where the heat is the greatest, because their most ardent wish is to be burned free of all self-absorption, and ultimately to disappear, into God's love. (The fire is consciousness.)

After his teacher died, Chao-chou remained in the monastery for a three-year mourning period; then he set out on a twenty-year pilgrimage to hone himself against the greatest Masters of his time. He said, in words that must have shocked the hierarchical and age-venerating Confucian mind, "If I meet a hundred-year-old man and I have something to teach him, I will teach; if I meet an eight-year-old boy and he has something to teach me, I will learn." Only when he was eighty years old did he feel mature enough to set up shop as a teacher. He taught for the next forty years, and his sayings are a marvel of lucidity, compassion, and humor.

Jesus must have undergone a good deal of spiritual development outside the story that has come down to us, before his enlightenment experience.

After it, there was still one place of vivid pain and darkness left in his heart, a residual sorrow from his childhood: one area of dust on an otherwise transparent windowpane. I will suggest that he later came, at least unconsciously, to a resolution of his family drama. But even if the dust remained, it doesn't detract from him. All of us have our assignments to complete, whether they are big or little. That Jesus was unclear on one point, that he couldn't yet fulfill the commandment to honor father and mother, shouldn't be shocking, even for devout Christians. "Therefore he had to become like his fellow humans in every way," the author of the Epistle to the Hebrews says. He was so young when he died. And he had such little time.

From this perspective, then, of relative and complete clarity, I would like to examine Jesus' relationship with his family.

Just as there is no mother in the parable of the Prodigal Son, Mary of Nazareth is almost completely absent from Jesus' life and words. When she does appear, once, in the authentic accounts of him, the incident is a painful one. The few times that he mentions her, his words are cool, even hostile. Here again, the evidence is scattered across the

Gospels; it needs to be assembled before we can see the connections.

To begin with, the relevant verses:

• When someone says to Jesus, "Your mother and your brothers are outside, asking for you," he refuses to let them enter the house and says, pointing to his disciples, "*These* are my mother and brothers. Whoever does the will of God is my brother, and sister, and mother." This statement is usually seen as an admirable instance of Jesus' fellowship with the community of believers. It may be that; but it is also, and primarily, I think, a rejection of his actual mother and brothers.

• When a woman in a crowd calls out, "Blessed is the womb that bore you and the breasts that gave you suck," Jesus says, "No: blessed rather are those who hear the word of God and obey it." Again, there may be a lesson here for the pious. But we can hear the subtext, and we can almost feel Jesus bristling at the woman's remark.

• He laments that "a prophet is not rejected [dishonored, treated with contempt] except in his own town and in his own family and in his own house."

• His teaching about loyalty to parents is uniformly negative, and is so shocking, not only to religious sensibilities but to our ordinary sense of decency, that it is almost never mentioned in church. When it *is* mentioned, it is softened, interpreted, and bent into an appropriately pious shape. But Jesus' words themselves are unambiguous:

> And as they were traveling along the road, he said to a certain man, "Follow me."
>
> And the man said, "Let me first go and bury my father."
>
> But Jesus said to him, "Let the dead bury their dead." [That is, "Let the spiritually dead bury their relatives who are physically dead."]
>
> Another man said to Jesus, "I will follow you, sir, but let me first say good-bye to my family."
>
> And Jesus said to him, "No one who puts his hand to the plow and then looks back is ready for the kingdom of God."

Jesus' point here is that we have to be ready to give up everything if we want to enter the kingdom of God. That is quite true. He said the same thing elsewhere, wonderfully, in his image of the merchant who found the pearl of great price and went and sold everything he had and bought it. What is shocking here is his timing: the words "Let the dead bury their dead," addressed to a man whose father has just died, are like a slap in the face. Even

Job's comforters knew when to remain silent. And surely Jesus could have allowed the second man to say good-bye to his wife and children.

This teaching about cutting off all family ties is epitomized by a verse in Luke: "If anyone comes to me and doesn't hate his own father and mother and wife and children and brothers and sisters and even his own life, he can't be my disciple." The sentiment is even stronger in a verse (with a Gnostic spin on it) from the Gospel of Thomas: "Whoever doesn't hate his father and his mother as I do can't become my disciple. And whoever doesn't love his true Father [God] and his true Mother [the Holy Spirit] as I do can't become my disciple. For my mother gave me death, but my true Mother gave me life."

The fairest and most positive summary of this aspect of Jesus' teaching was made by George Bernard Shaw, of all people:

> Get rid of your family entanglements. Every mother you meet is as much your mother as the woman who bore you. Every man you meet is as much your brother as the man she bore after you. Don't waste your time at family funerals grieving for your relatives: attend to life, not

death: there are as good fish in the sea as ever came out of it, and better. In the kingdom of heaven, which, as aforesaid, is within you, there is no marriage nor giving in marriage, because you cannot devote your life to two divinities: God and the person you are married to.

All this is true in a certain way, true for certain people or at certain stages of life. It is especially appropriate for young adults, who often need a moratorium to sort out their various confusions, and for those extremely rare people who have arrived at a sense of wholeness with their sexuality and want to devote themselves to a life of contemplation. But it is also untrue. However much I see all women as my mothers, I have a special bond with my flesh-and-blood mother, and if I don't honor it with my full attention, the flow of my love will be obstructed, and a portion of my heart will remain opaque. Nor is it true to say that in the kingdom of heaven there is no marriage. Marriage is one of the most direct paths to and in the kingdom of heaven. When I can truly devote myself to my wife, I *am* devoting myself to God, because all love is the love of God. "For the mature person," wrote Tzu-ssu, "the Tao begins in the relation between man and woman, and ends in the infinite vastness of the universe."

Of course, many men, in many religious traditions, have felt a powerful conflict between family life and religious life; that is why celibacy has traditionally been seen as the most direct path to God. But, as anyone who reads Paul or Augustine knows, it is one thing to give up sex with your body and quite another to give it up in your mind. In the same way, it is one thing to leave your parents and quite another to let go of them in your mind. Abraham is the symbol for the latter, complete liberation: because he is able to leave his father's house forever, he is given an eternal blessing from God.

A couple of months after I began studying with my old Zen Master, he said to me, "You have three jobs here. Your first job is to kill the Buddha." I had read that phrase in the old Zen teachings, and I knew what it meant—to let go of any concepts of a separate, superior, enlightened being outside myself. Then he said, "Your second job is to kill your parents."

"What does that mean?" I asked.

"As long as there is anything you want from your parents," he said, "or anything about them that upsets you, they will be an obstacle in your mind. 'Killing your parents' means accepting them just as they are. They enter your mind like an image reflected on the water. No ripples."

"It sounds very difficult."

"Only if you think it is," he said.

Then he said, "Your third job is to kill me."

It is, in fact, possible to leave everything without leaving anything. We learn this from the teachings of the great Masters, and we can know it for ourselves, through our own experience. It is only for people in the more arduous stages of transformation that there is a conflict. Even when we understand the concern for wholeheartedness that caused Jesus to teach as he did about family, we can recognize an extreme quality, a lack of balance, an off-centeredness, in the tone of these sayings that almost begs us to consider them in the realm not of spiritual teaching but of psychology.

The clearest statements I have found about attachment to home and family occur in the teaching of Ramana Maharshi. A beginner once said to him, "I want to give up my job and family and stay with you, sir, so that I can be with God." Maharshi said, "God is always with you, in you. That is what you should realize."

Questioner: But I feel the urge to give up all attachments and renounce the world.

Maharshi: Renunciation doesn't mean giving away your money or abandoning your home. True renunciation is the renunciation of desires, passions, and attachments.

Questioner: But single-minded devotion to God may not be possible unless one leaves worldly things.

Maharshi: No: a true renunciate actually merges in the world and expands his love to embrace the whole world. It would be more correct to describe the attitude of the devotee as universal love than as abandoning home to become a monk.

Questioner: At home the bonds of affection are too strong.

Maharshi: If you renounce home when you aren't ripe for it, you only create new bonds.

Questioner: Isn't renunciation the supreme means of breaking attachments?

Maharshi: That may be so for someone whose mind is already free from entanglements. But you haven't grasped the deeper meaning of renunciation. Great souls who have abandoned their homes have done so not out of aversion to family life, but because of their largehearted and all-embracing love for all mankind and all creatures.

Questioner: Family ties will have to be left behind sometime, so why shouldn't I take the initiative and break them now, so that my love can be equal toward all people?

Maharshi: When you truly feel this equal love for all, when your heart has expanded so much that it embraces the whole of creation, you will certainly not feel like giving up this or that. You will simply drop off from secular life as a ripe fruit drops from the branch of a tree. You will feel that the whole world is your home.

I have already quoted a verse from the one incident in which Mary appears. This incident requires closer attention. It begins with one of the most hair-raising verses in the Gospels:

And when his family heard [about all this], they went to seize him, for they said, "He is out of his mind."

Hidden inside this verse is a world of misunderstanding and disappointment. Actually, it is a miracle that the verse survived at all, to speak to us. It appears only in Mark; both Matthew and Luke apparently found it so shocking that they deleted it from their accounts. (Even in Mark, the transcribers of two of the best ancient manuscripts were so embarrassed by it that they altered it to read, "And when *the scribes and the others* heard about him, they went to seize him, for they said, 'He is out of his mind.'")

What is happening here? We can't be certain of the details, because we don't know what Mary and Jesus' brothers heard that troubled them so much. Perhaps it had to do with his healings and exorcisms at Capernaum; perhaps a neighbor had watched one of the treatments and had returned to Nazareth with a frightened report about the strange sounds Jesus had uttered or the physical contortions he had gone through. Or perhaps there were rumors of his bizarre and incomprehensible doctrines: that the pure in heart can actually see God, or that adults should be like children, or that the kingdom of God has already come. Whatever it was that they heard, they concluded that he had gone insane. So, like any responsible family, concerned for his well-being and wanting to prevent him from harming himself or others, they went out to "seize" him and bring him back home (the Greek

verb is a strong one, and is used later in Mark, of
the troops in Gethsemane, with the meaning "to
arrest").

And his mother and his brothers arrived, and
standing outside, they sent in a message asking
for him.

And people in the crowd sitting around him
said to him, "Your mother and your brothers are
outside and want to see you."

And Jesus said, "Who are my mother and my
brothers?" And looking at those who sat in a circle around him, he said, "*These* are my mother
and my brothers. Whoever does the will of God
is my brother, and sister, and mother."

When Jesus' mother and brothers arrive at Capernaum, he is in a house, teaching, with a crowd of
disciples and sympathizers around him. The crowd
is so large that Mary and the brothers can't enter, so
they send in a message, asking him to come out;
their intention is to "seize" him and take him home
to Nazareth. When he is told that they are waiting
for him, Jesus' response is, in effect, to disown
them. Of course, it isn't difficult to see Jesus' point:
that he loves those who do God's will more than he
loves even his own mother (if she were not to do

God's will). We can realize the truth of this teaching, on the absolute level—it is true in the same sense in which the primal commandment to love God with *all* one's heart is true—and at the same time recognize, on the relative level, the lack of wholeness, of healedness, in its antagonistic tone. This note of irritation was already pointed out by the heretic Mani in the fourth-century *Debates of Archelaus, Bishop of Mesopotamia, and the Heresiarch Mani*:

> Mani said, "Someone once said to Jesus, 'Your mother and your brothers are outside,' and Jesus did not kindly receive the person who said this, but indignantly rebuked him, saying, 'Who are my mother and my brothers?'"

Christian scholars have felt such a compelling need to justify Jesus' conduct that they haven't really taken it in. The Jewish scholar C. G. Montefiore is more objective, though in his comment there is an element of blame:

> It has been urged that the harsh bearing of Jesus towards his mother and family may be explained and justified on the grounds (a) that his family did not understand or believe in his mission, (b)

that his whole soul was so filled with this mission that there was no room in it for family ties and interests, and (c) (the most important of all) that his special work implied and demanded a separation from, an abandonment of, all worldly connections and occupations.

Yet when all is said, there is a certain violation or *froissement* of Jewish sentiment as to parents in this passage, and it is strange to find Jesus, who acts so dubiously towards his own mother, afterwards [Mark 7:9ff.] reproaching the Pharisees with not honoring father and mother! Even if the explanations of his conduct given above are adequate, Jesus might have explained matters to his mother and family quietly and in private, whereas he, in order to score a point, put them to open shame and humiliation. . . . No Jew who remains a Jew can well believe that the conduct of Jesus in this story, however justified in its essential issues, was justified in detail, blameless and exquisite in method.

But there is no reason to blame Jesus for his conduct. What is important is to see it clearly. His rejection of his mother seems to me an early, inadequate response to what he must have felt as her rejection of him, her incomprehension of who he had become. Or perhaps it goes back further, to his childhood. Perhaps it contains an unconscious or half-conscious element of blame for the stigma of his birth, and was part of his distancing himself from his shame and everything connected with it.

When someone undergoes a spiritual transformation, he or she is truly reborn. The shape of the personality may be the same, and a residue of unfinished karmic business may still be there, but in the depths, the old, self-preoccupied self is dead and there is a wholly new awareness. Integration of this new self into one's life and family and society is the greatest and most difficult challenge in spiritual practice. (The work may take seven years or seven lifetimes, but people who are in love with God do it gladly; as in the story of Jacob and Rachel, the years "seemed to him only a few days, so great was his love for her.") It is particularly difficult with parents, who are deeply invested in creating us in their own image, and see only the former self who was their child. How can they understand that one's roots have grown deeper than the family, have penetrated beyond birth and death? Incomprehension is a given, except in very rare instances. The question is how one deals with the incomprehension.

While no other great spiritual teacher I know of had to face such a difficult childhood as Jesus did, all others had to give up their attachments to personal relationships, especially to the powerful centrifugal force of the family. Departures are often painful, and those who are left behind feel betrayed or abandoned. We can't help that. But if, like Abraham, we live in the place from which it is impossible to depart, we can make our departure an act of love. We are "ahead of all parting," as Rilke put it, and not only for ourselves. How poignant is the moment in the life of the Buddha when Gautama, knowing he has to leave his beloved wife and set out to solve the great question of life and death, leans over her sleeping body and kisses her on the cheek, one last time. But if he hadn't left, he could never have awakened and helped countless others to awaken, including her.

Jesus' return to his family after his baptism experience must have been as painful as his subsequent return to Nazareth. We have an account of the latter, and it is a story of rejection:

From there he went to Nazareth, his native town, and his disciples followed him.

And when the Sabbath came, he began to

teach in the synagogue, and many people who
heard him were bewildered, and said, "Where
does this fellow get such stuff?" and "What
makes *him* so wise?" and "How can he be a
miracle-worker? Isn't this the carpenter, Mary's
bastard, the brother of James and Joseph and
Judas and Simon, and aren't his sisters here with
us?" And they were prevented from believing in
him.

And Jesus said, "A prophet is not rejected
except in his own town and in his own family
and in his own house."

And he was unable to do any miracle there,
because of their disbelief.

In this story, the people of Nazareth can't believe
that the Jesus whom they knew as an illegitimate
child has been transformed into a prophet. They
see him through the distorting lens of the past, and
therefore are completely unaware of his presence.
We aren't told whether Mary or any of Jesus'
brothers or sisters were in the synagogue on this
occasion. But the reaction of the townspeople is
similar to the family's reaction. (In a different context, the Gospel of John says that "even his own
brothers didn't believe in him.")

There is a striking comment on the Nazareth incident by Zen Master Ma-tsu (709–788), who of course had never heard of Jesus:

> Don't return to your native town:
> you can't teach the truth there.
> By the village stream an old woman
> is calling you by your childhood name.

This little poem is both lovely and poignant in its acceptance of a psychological given: that even the greatest Master may still appear to his family as the child he was—small, needy, untransformed.

With both his family and the people of Nazareth, Jesus' reaction is to depart and shake off the dust from his feet. But this seems to me a provisional attitude, and I think he held to it as a matter of protection, while he was coming to full inner ripeness. There is a traditional Hindu metaphor that clarifies two appropriate stages:

> When the young plant is just sprouting out of the seed or is still weak and tender, it requires seclusion and the protection of a strong thorny fence to keep off cattle that might otherwise eat it or trample upon and destroy it. But the same shoot, when it develops into a large tree, dis-

penses with such protection and itself affords shade, sustenance, and protection to cattle and men, without detriment to itself.

At this later stage, detachment and filial piety aren't mutually exclusive. When someone has found freedom in his heart, everything that was once an obstacle—parents, money, sex—becomes an opportunity for a further degree of surrender. We can sense this freedom in Jesus' parables, when he speaks of Samaritans and sinners. And we feel that someone as largehearted and compassionate as he was would surely have been able to fulfill both the commandment to love God with all his heart and the commandment to honor his mother. John the Evangelist was so convinced of this that he imagines Mary at the foot of the Cross, and imagines Jesus, in almost his final words, placing her in the care of the "disciple whom he loved." That is what gives his account a sense of personal closure that the other three Gospels don't have. When we love someone, we wish him all possible peace and wholeness in his heart. And we want him, before he dies, to have finished his earthly business, which is, after all, his Father's business as well.

VIII

Before I return to Jesus and Mary, I would like to say a little more about forgiveness.

It is Jesus' most important teaching for those who aren't ready to enter the kingdom of God, as Blake recognized:

> There is not one moral virtue that Jesus inculcated but Plato and Cicero did inculcate before him. What then did Christ inculcate? Forgiveness of sins. This alone is the gospel and this is the life and immortality brought to light by Jesus, even the covenant of Jehovah, which is this: if you forgive one another your trespasses, so shall Jehovah forgive you, that he himself may dwell among you.

Forgiveness is a sign pointing us toward that kingdom. We ask Jesus, *How should we live?* He says, *Love God, love your neighbor.* We ask, *What is that like?* He says, *Let go.* Letting go of an offense means letting go of the self that is offended.

There are only a few passages in which Jesus mentions forgiveness, but they are central. In all of them, he is teaching *us* forgiveness; it is never a question of *his* forgiving sins. The two passages in which Jesus himself is said to forgive sins — the stories of the man sick with palsy, and of the repentant sinner who wets Jesus' feet with her tears — probably derive from the church's image of him as a divine being. The most that Jesus could have taught these two unhappy people would be to forgive themselves. Or he could have said, as a provisional teaching, that God had forgiven them. But actually, forgiveness is an experience that happens only outside the kingdom of God. If you have to let go, then there was something to hold on to. Where there is no offense to begin with, there is nothing to forgive. It is more accurate to say that inside the kingdom of God there is only acceptance.

In Jesus' sayings, it may seem as if God's forgiveness is dependent on ours. "Forgive us our wrongs, as we forgive those who have wronged us." "For if you forgive others their offenses, your heavenly Father will forgive you." "If you don't judge, you will not be judged; if you don't condemn, you will not be condemned; if you forgive, you will be forgiven." But these *if*s have only one side, like a Möbius strip. Jesus doesn't mean that if you do condemn, God will condemn *you*; or that if you don't forgive, God won't forgive *you*. He is pointing to a spiritual fact: when we condemn, we create a world of condemnation for ourselves, and we attract the condemnation of others; when we cling to an offense, we are clinging to precisely what separates us from our own fulfillment. Letting go means not only releasing the person who has wronged us, but releasing ourselves. A place opens up inside us where that person is always welcome, and where we can always meet her again, face to face.

In these sayings of Jesus, God is a mirror reflecting back to us our own state of being. We receive exactly what we give. The more openhearted we are, the more we can experience the whole universe as God's grace. Forgiveness is essentially openness of heart. It is an attitude, not an action.

Peter once asked him, "Sir, how often should I forgive my brother if he keeps wronging me? Up to seven times?"

And Jesus said to him, "Not just seven: seventy times seven."

It doesn't arise from morality, but from vision; it doesn't require effort, but is itself the inexhaustible energy of life.

> Why did the ancient Masters esteem the Tao?
> Because, being one with the Tao,
> when you seek, you find;
> and when you make a mistake, you are forgiven.
> That is why everybody loves it.
>
> *Tao Te Ching*, 62

This is the vivid experience of everyone who lives in harmony with the way things are. What does it mean to say that when we are at one with the Tao we are forgiven? As soon as we make a mistake, we become aware of it, we admit it, and we correct it, on the spot. Thus there is no residue.

Attitude precedes action and generates it. The Buddhists are particularly adept at cultivating the mind of universal compassion, and have a scripture, the Metta Sutta (the Scripture of Lovingkindness), which could be seen as a meticulous commentary on the above-quoted verse from the Lord's Prayer: "Forgive us our wrongs, as we forgive those who have wronged us." It includes a directed meditation in which the meditator is asked to open his heart and, first, forgive himself for any wrong he has ever committed, in thought, word, or deed. Then he is asked to forgive anyone who has ever wronged him and to let go of the offense completely. Finally he is asked to send lovingkindness to his enemies and all those he dislikes, and to all beings in the universe, humans and animals and plants and paramecia and all other unimaginable life forms, and to wish them perfect joy. (Anyone who finds it difficult to forgive should try the effects of doing this meditation every day, for ten or twenty years.)

Jesus' most profound and moving statement on forgiveness is, again, the parable of the Prodigal Son. There is no explicit mention of forgiveness in it. But its point is obvious: the father's heart has always been open. When he runs to embrace the younger son, he is not *doing* anything; he is simply expressing what he has always felt. And once the son returns, he doesn't have to do a thing to earn his father's forgiveness. Forgiveness is already fully there, in the embrace, before the son can even open his mouth to beg it.

This teaching about forgiveness is not new to Judaism, but in the parable of the Prodigal Son it is stated with the greatest clarity and depth. As with any image or metaphor that tries to illuminate a three-dimensional human truth, the light shines on just one side. Jesus' emphasis is on the father's joy, which we can feel bursting through every vessel in his body as he forgets his patriarchal dignity and rushes out to welcome his returning son.

The prophets illuminate another side. They portray Israel as a wife, and God as a husband who forgives her. In Second Isaiah, the wife has been abandoned for a long time (we aren't told why); but God ultimately has compassion on her and takes her back "with eternal love." Jeremiah's image is more detailed, and more shocking: Israel has betrayed God and is like an unfaithful wife; she has been promiscuous; she has acted like a whore. But God's love, says Jeremiah, is unfailing. Though Israel has been unfaithful, God is not unfaithful. If only Israel will return to him, he will take her into his arms again, as a beloved wife.

The prophets' image doesn't express the profound joy that we feel in Jesus' image of the father. But the father hasn't been wronged directly and personally, as the God of the prophets has. The aspect of the truth which this image illuminates is that God's love, and therefore ours, can forgive anything. Imagine the worst offense possible: imagine being betrayed by the person you loved and trusted the most, imagine the most painful sexual wound you can possibly experience. Even this, the prophets are saying, can be transformed into absolute forgiveness. All Israel, all each of us, needs to do is to return to the love that is always ready to receive us.

The most powerful of the prophetic images occurs at the beginning of Hosea. "Go take a whore as your wife," God tells the prophet abruptly. The voice comes out of nowhere. There is no prologue, and only the starkest of explanations to soften the shock and urgency of the command. "Marry her and have children with her, because this land has acted like a whore." Here the image is hair-raising not only because of its savage bluntness but, even more, because its intent is not to stay in the realm of images. Hosea is commanded to enact it; the word has to become flesh. In surrendering everything, he allows his whole life to become a metaphor. And eventually, through his love for his unfaithful wife, he is able to fathom God's forgiveness in the depths of his own heart, and to become its perfect embodiment.

"I will marry you to myself forever; I will marry
you to myself in righteousness and justice, in
love and compassion; I will marry you to myself
in faithfulness; and you will know the Unnamable."

IX

In Jesus' sayings, and in his one recorded meeting
with his mother, it is apparent that he hasn't yet forgiven her. His gruffness, his resistance to anything
that has to do with family, indicate that he hasn't
let go.

We have no explicit information about how or
whether he came to a more mature resolution of
the relationship. In the Synoptic Gospels, Mary
simply disappears from the picture.

But there is a hint: the story of the Woman
Caught in Adultery.

The next morning, as Jesus was teaching in the
Temple, the scribes brought a woman who had
been caught in adultery, and they stood her in
the middle. And they said to him, "Rabbi, this
woman was caught in adultery, in the very act.

Moses in the Law commanded us to stone such women to death; what do *you* say?"

But Jesus stooped down and with his finger wrote on the ground.

And as they continued to question him, he stood up and said to them, "Let whoever of you is sinless be the first to throw a stone at her." And again he stooped down and wrote on the ground.

And when they heard this, they went out one by one, the older ones first. And Jesus was left alone, with the woman still standing there.

And Jesus stood up, and said to her, "Woman, where are they? Has no one condemned you?"

And she said, "No one, sir."

And Jesus said, "I don't condemn you either. Go now, and sin no more."

This famous passage has the strangest history of any text in the Gospels. It doesn't appear in any of the most ancient manuscripts, and seems to have been circulating as a free-floating piece of oral tradition until the end of the fourth century, when it began to be added to the written Gospels. Most scribes ineptly tacked it on to the Gospel of John, after 7:52 (this is where it appears in the Textus Receptus, and hence in the King James version), though some placed it after 7:36 or 7:44 or 21:25. One insightful scribe placed it after Luke 21:38, recognizing that the passage is written in a style very different from John's, and more like Luke's. On external evidence, then, the story has only a shaky claim to authenticity. Nevertheless, the best scholars agree that it "has all the earmarks of historical veracity."

Three details seem to me especially convincing. The first is Jesus' gesture of writing on the ground, which has eluded scholars and theologians for at least sixteen centuries. The very fact that it has no obvious meaning is evidence for its authenticity, since subtlety of this kind is never present in the church's stories, in which "Jesus" becomes more and more supernatural as the decades go on. I can't imagine any disciple inventing a Jesus who has to think and doodle on the ground. This gesture was, in fact, so irritating or baffling to Christian exegetes that they converted it into another superhuman display: according to them, what Jesus wrote on the ground was the sins of all the accusing scribes.

The second detail is the statement "Let whoever of you is sinless be the first to throw a stone at her." Here Jesus is including himself with all human beings, as capable of making mistakes. He is certainly not saying, "Only I, who am sinless, have the right to throw a stone at her," but rather "None of us has the right." Blake, in "The Everlasting Gospel," makes this point explicit by prefacing it with Jesus' statement in Mark 10:18 that "No one is good except God alone":

> "Thou [God] art good and Thou alone,
> Nor may the sinner cast one stone."

The third detail is the final statement, "I don't condemn you either." If this were a creation of the early church, like Luke's story of the repentant sinner, it would have had Jesus say, "Your sins are forgiven," and make the story's focal point the doctrine that "the Son of Man has the authority on earth to forgive sins." Here, Jesus correctly understands that forgiveness is not the issue, since the woman has committed no offense against him. "I don't condemn you" doesn't mean "I forgive you." Only her husband was in a position to forgive her, since only he was wronged.

In the story of the adulteress, Jesus is brought face to face with a woman who symbolically and psychologically stands for his mother. She too has committed adultery, and he is being asked to judge her. Since our attitudes and actions toward people of the opposite sex are a reflection of our unconscious attitudes toward our parent of the opposite sex, I feel that Jesus couldn't have treated the adulteress as he did, with love and absolute nonjudgment, if he hadn't first, somewhere in his depths, forgiven Mary. If such a transformation took place, before this incident or during it, it was as important as the one he underwent at his baptism. There, he felt forgiven by his Father; here, he was able to forgive his mother. And if the one insightful scribe was correct in placing the incident after Luke 21:38, it has even greater significance. It is the last event we are told about in the authentic accounts of Jesus, before his arrest and crucifixion. It may have been the last teaching he ever gave.

When John the Evangelist has Jesus look down from the cross and place his mother in the care of the "disciple whom he loved," he is describing a scene which has no basis in historical reality, a scene imagined by his own very touching piety, out of his desire for it to be true. Perhaps that is what I have done here. Perhaps the story of the adulteress never actually took place. Or if it did, it is possible that Jesus was able to see her with a nonjudgmental love and still, in some hidden corner of his heart, keep holding on to his rejection of his mother.

But I don't think that someone who had experienced forgiveness as Jesus had, someone whose teachings about it have the depth and beauty that his teachings do, would himself have been unable to forgive. If this story gives us no historical information, it can nevertheless serve as a symbolic reminder of how we must come to peace with parents, lovers, friends and enemies, and with the most difficult, unlovable parts of ourselves. The more fully we accept them and thus let them go, the more light we allow into our hearts. And as Paul said about each of us, in one of his most transparent insights, "When all things are made whole in the Son, then he will be wholly included in the Father, so that God may be All in all."

THE GOSPEL

I

This is the book of the good news that Jesus of Nazareth proclaimed.

John the Baptizer appeared in the wilderness, proclaiming a baptism of renewal for the forgiveness of sins. And John was clothed in camel's hair, with a belt of animal hide around his waist, and he ate locusts and wild honey. And people from all of Judea went out to him, and many people from Jerusalem, and they were baptized by him in the Jordan River, confessing their sins.

And at that time Jesus came from Nazareth in Galilee, and was baptized in the Jordan by John.

And afterward the Spirit drove him out into the wilderness. And he was in the wilderness for forty days, with the wild animals.

2

And when Jesus heard that John had been arrested, he withdrew to Galilee, and leaving Nazareth, he settled in Capernaum by the lake. And he began to teach and proclaim the good news of the kingdom of God.

And as he was walking beside the Sea of Galilee, he saw Simon and his brother Andrew casting a fishing net into the lake. And Jesus said to them, "Come, follow me." And immediately they left their nets and followed him.

And walking on a little farther, he saw James the son of Zebedee and John his brother, who were in their boat mending their nets. And he called them, and immediately they left their father Zebedee in the boat with the hired men and followed him.

And they came to Capernaum. And on the Sabbath, Jesus went into the synagogue and taught. And people were astonished at his

teaching, for he taught them like someone who has authority, and not like the scribes.

And when they left the synagogue, they went to the house of Simon and Andrew, along with James and John. And Simon's mother-in-law was in bed with a fever. And as soon as they told Jesus about her, he went and took her by the hand and lifted her up, and the fever left her, and she served them.

And that evening, they brought to him everyone who was sick or insane, and the whole village was gathered at the door, and he healed many people.

And early in the morning, while it was still dark, he got up and went out to a remote place and prayed there. And Simon and his companions searched for him, and when they found him, they said to him, "Everyone is looking for you." And he said to them, "Let us go on to the next villages, so that I can proclaim the good news there too."

And he went through all of Galilee, pro-

claiming the good news in their synagogues and healing many diseases.

And in one of the villages, a leper came and knelt before him and said, "If you wish, you can cleanse me."

And Jesus, moved with compassion, stretched out his hand and touched him and said, "I do wish it; be cleansed."

And immediately the leprosy left him, and he was cleansed.

And Jesus said to him, "Go and show yourself to the priest and offer for your cleansing what Moses commanded."

And the man went out and began to talk about it excitedly, and the news spread, until Jesus could no longer go into a village, but had to stay out in the countryside. And people came to him from every direction.

3

And he went again to the lakeside, and began to teach, and so many people gathered that he

had to get into a boat on the lake. And he sat in it, and the whole crowd sat on the shore, up to the water's edge.

And he taught them many things in parables, and said, "What is the kingdom of God like? It is like a man who sows a seed on the earth: he goes about his business, and day by day the seed sprouts and grows, he doesn't know how. The earth bears fruit by itself, first the stalk, then the ear, then the full grain in the ear. And when the grain is ripe, the man goes in with his sickle, because it is harvest time.

"The kingdom of God is like a mustard seed, which is smaller than any other seed; but when it is sown, it grows up and becomes the largest of shrubs, and puts forth large branches, so that the birds of the sky are able to make their nests in its shade.

"The kingdom of God is like yeast, which a woman took and mixed in with fifty pounds of dough, until all of it was leavened.

"The kingdom of God is like a treasure buried in a field, which a man found and bur-

ied again; then in his joy he goes and sells everything he has and buys that field.

"Or the kingdom of God is like this: there was a merchant looking for fine pearls, who found one pearl of great price, and he went and sold everything he had and bought it.

"Thus, every scribe who has been trained for the kingdom of God is like a householder who can bring forth out of his treasure room both the new and the old."

And someone asked him, "When will the kingdom of God come?"

And he said, "The kingdom of God will not come if you watch for it. Nor will anyone be able to say, 'It is here' or 'It is there.' For the kingdom of God is within you."

And he said, "When you light a lamp, do you put it under a basket or under a bed? Don't you put it on a lampstand? For there is nothing hidden that can't be made clear, and nothing secret that can't become obvious. Pay attention to what you hear; the measure you give is the measure you receive."

4

Another time, Jesus was walking beside the lake, and a crowd gathered around him, and he taught them. And as he walked on, he saw Levi the son of Alphaeus sitting at the tax booth, and he said to him, "Follow me." And he stood up and followed him.

And many people who held the Law in contempt began to follow Jesus. And the scribes said to him, "Why do you eat with traitors and whores?" And Jesus said to them, "It isn't the healthy who need a doctor, but the sick. My teaching is not meant for those who are already righteous, but for the wicked."

And he went up into the hills and called his disciples and appointed twelve of them to be with him and to be sent out to proclaim the

kingdom of God and to heal: Simon, whom he named Peter, James the son of Zebedee and John his brother, whom he named *B'nai-rogez* (which means "sons of thunder"), Andrew, and Philip, and Bartholomew, and Matthew, and Thomas, and James the son of Alphaeus, and Thaddaeus, and Simon the Zealot, and Judas Iscariot.

And he went through all the towns and villages, teaching in their synagogues, and proclaiming the good news of the kingdom of God. And the Twelve went with him, and also certain women whom he had cured of diseases and infirmities: Mary of Magdala, who had been insane, and Joanna the wife of Herod's steward Kooza, and Susannah, and many others, who provided for them out of their own resources. And his fame spread throughout the surrounding region of Galilee, and people brought the sick on stretchers to wherever they heard he was staying, and whenever he came to a town or village, they would lay down the sick in the marketplace. And they

brought him those who were suffering from many kinds of diseases and torments, and demoniacs, and epileptics, and paralytics, and he healed them.

And after Jesus returned to Capernaum, people heard that he was at home; and so many gathered in the house that there was no room, not even in front of the door.

And as he was teaching, some people brought a paralytic to him, carried by four men. And when they couldn't get near him because of the crowd, they made a hole in the roof over the place where Jesus was, and they lowered the mat, with the paralytic lying on it, through the hole.

And when Jesus saw how deeply they trusted him, he said to the paralytic, "Stand up, child; take your mat and go home."

And immediately the man stood up and took the mat and walked out of the house in front of everyone. And they were all amazed, and glorified God and said, "We have never seen anything like this!"

5

And large crowds followed him from Galilee and the Decapolis and Jerusalem and Judea and beyond the Jordan. And seeing the crowds, he went up onto a hill, and when he had sat down, his disciples gathered around him. And he began to teach them, and said,

"Blessed are the poor in spirit, for theirs is the kingdom of God.

"Blessed are those who grieve, for they will be comforted.

"Blessed are those who hunger and thirst for righteousness, for they will be filled.

"Blessed are the merciful, for they will receive mercy.

"Blessed are the pure in heart, for they will see God.

"Blessed are the peacemakers, for they will be called sons of God.

"No one lights a lamp and then puts it under a basket, but on a lampstand, and it gives light to everyone in the house. In the same way, let your light shine before men, so that they may see your good works and glorify your Father in heaven.

"Don't think that my purpose is to destroy the law; my purpose is not to destroy the law but to fulfill it. For I tell you that unless your righteousness is deeper than the righteousness of the scribes, you will never enter the kingdom of God.

"You have heard that it was said to our forefathers, *You shall not murder* and *Whoever murders is liable to judgment.* But I tell you that anyone who hates his brother will be liable to judgment.

"You have heard that it was said, *You shall not commit adultery.* But I tell you that anyone who harbors lust for a woman has already committed adultery with her in his heart.

"You have heard that it was said, *You shall not perjure yourselves.* But I tell you, don't take any oaths at all. Let your 'Yes' mean 'Yes' and your 'No' mean 'No.'

"You have heard that it was said, *An eye for*

an eye and a tooth for a tooth. But I tell you, don't resist a wicked man. If anyone hits you on one cheek, turn the other cheek to him also. And if anyone wants to sue you and take your shirt, let him have your coat as well. And if a soldier forces you into service for one mile, go two miles with him. Give to everyone who asks, and don't refuse anyone who wants to borrow from you.

"You have heard that it was said, *You shall love your neighbor.* But I tell you, love your enemies, do good to those who hate you, bless those who curse you, and pray for those who mistreat you, so that you may be sons of your Father in heaven; for he makes his sun rise on the wicked and on the good, and sends rain to the righteous and to the unrighteous.

"For if you love only those who love you, what credit is that to you: don't even the tax-gatherers do the same? And if you do good only to those who do good to you: don't even the Gentiles do the same? But love your enemies, and give, expecting nothing in return;

and your reward will be great, and you will be sons of the Most High, for he is kind even to the ungrateful and the wicked. Therefore be merciful, just as your Father is merciful.

"Be careful not to do your righteous acts in public, in order to be seen. When you give charity, don't blow a trumpet to announce it, as the hypocrites do in the synagogues and in the streets, so that people will praise them. Truly I tell you, they have their reward. But when you give charity, don't let your left hand know what your right hand is doing, and keep your charity a secret; and your Father, who sees what is secret, will reward you.

"And when you pray, don't be like the hypocrites, who love to stand and pray in the synagogues and the street corners, so that people will see them. But when you pray, go into your inner room and shut the door and pray in secret to your Father; and your Father, who sees what is secret, will reward you.

"And in your prayers, don't talk on and on, as the Gentiles do; for they think that unless

they use many words they won't be heard.
Don't be like them, for your Father knows
what you need even before you ask him. But
pray like this:

> Our Father in heaven,
>> hallowed be your name.
> May your kingdom come,
>> may your will be done
>> on earth as it is in heaven.
> Give us this day our daily bread,
>> and forgive us our wrongs
>> as we forgive those who have wronged us.
> And do not lead us into temptation,
>> but deliver us from evil.

For if you forgive others their offenses, your
heavenly Father will forgive you.

"The eye is the lamp of the body. So if your
eye is clear, your whole body is luminous; but
if your eye isn't clear, your whole body is dark.
And if the light in you is darkness, how great
that darkness is.

"Can a blind man lead a blind man? Won't

they both fall into a ditch? A disciple is not above his teacher, but every disciple who is fully taught will be like his teacher."

6

"Ask, and it will be given to you; seek, and you will find; knock, and the door will be opened to you. For everyone who asks, receives; and he who seeks, finds; and to him who knocks, the door will be opened.

"What man among you, when his son asks him for a loaf of bread, will give him a stone; or when he asks for a fish, will give him a snake? If you, then, who are imperfect, know how to give good gifts to your children, how much more will your Father, who is perfect, give good things to those who ask him.

"Therefore I tell you, don't be anxious about what you will eat or what you will wear. Isn't your life more than its food, and your body more than its clothing? Look at the birds of the sky: they neither sow nor reap nor gather into barns, yet God feeds them. Which of you by thinking can add a day to his life? And why do you worry about clothing? Consider the lilies of the field, how they grow: they neither toil nor spin. And yet I tell you that not even Solomon in all his glory was robed like one of these. Therefore, if God so clothes the grass, which grows in the field today, and tomorrow is thrown into the oven, won't he all the more clothe you? So don't worry about these things and say, 'What will we eat?' or 'What will we wear?' For that is what the Gentiles seek; and your Father knows that you need these things. But first seek the kingdom of God; and these things will be given to you as well.

"Aren't two sparrows sold for a penny? Yet not one of them falls to the ground apart from your Father. As for you, every hair on your head is numbered. So don't be afraid: you are worth more than many sparrows.

"Don't judge, and you will not be judged. For in the same way that you judge people, you yourself will be judged.

"Why do you see the splinter that is in your brother's eye, but don't notice the log that is in your own eye? First take the log out of your own eye, and then you will see clearly enough to take the splinter out of your brother's eye.

"So if you don't judge, you will not be judged; if you don't condemn, you will not be condemned; if you forgive, you will be forgiven; if you give, things will be given to you: good measure will be poured into your lap, pressed down, shaken together, and overflowing. For the measure by which you give is the measure by which you will receive.

"Therefore, whatever you want others to do to you, do to them. This is the essence of the Law and the prophets.

"Enter by the narrow gate. For the gate is wide and the way is easy that leads to suffering, and

those who go through it are many. But the gate is narrow and the way is hard that leads to true life, and those who find it are few.

"Everyone who hears what I say and does it is like a man who built his house upon rock; and the rain fell and the floods came and the winds blew and beat against that house, and it didn't fall, because it was founded on rock. And everyone who hears what I say and doesn't do it is like a man who built his house upon sand; and the rain fell and the floods came and the winds blew and beat against that house, and it fell; and great was its fall."

7

And when Jesus came down from the hill, he went to the lakeside with his disciples, and large crowds from Galilee followed; and large crowds, hearing of his works, came to him from Judea and Jerusalem as well, and from Idumea and beyond the Jordan and the region of Tyre and Sidon. And he told the disciples to have a boat ready for him, so that he wouldn't be crushed by the crowd, for he had healed many people, and the crippled and sick were all pressing in on him to touch him.

Then he went into the house; and such a large crowd gathered around them that they didn't even have time to eat.

And when his family heard about all this, they went to seize him, for they said, "He is out of his mind."

And a mute demoniac was brought to Jesus, and he healed him, and the man began to speak. And all the people were amazed.

But certain scribes who had come down from Jerusalem said, "He is possessed by Beelzebul" and "He casts out demons by using the prince of demons."

And his mother and his brothers arrived, and standing outside, they sent in a message asking for him.

And people in the crowd sitting around him said to him, "Your mother and your brothers are outside and want to see you."

And Jesus said, "Who are my mother and my brothers?" And looking at those who sat in a circle around him, he said, "*These* are my mother and my brothers. Whoever does the will of God is my brother, and sister, and mother."

Once, when Jesus had returned by boat from the other side of the lake, a large crowd gathered around him at the shore. And one of the leaders of the synagogue came to him and prostrated himself at his feet and said, "My little girl is near death; come, I beg of you, lay your hands on her and save her life."

And Jesus went with him. And a large crowd followed and pressed in on him.

And there was a woman in the crowd who had been bleeding for a dozen years, and she had been treated by many doctors, and had spent all her money, and hadn't gotten better

but worse. And she had heard about Jesus, and she came up behind him in the crowd and touched his robe, for she thought, "If I touch even his clothes, I will be healed." And immediately the bleeding dried up, and she knew in her body that she was cured of the disease.

And immediately Jesus felt in himself that power had gone forth from him, and he turned around in the crowd and said, "Who touched my clothes?"

And his disciples said to him, "You see the crowd pressing in on you; why do you ask, 'Who touched me?'"

And he looked around to see who had done it.

And the woman, frightened and trembling, knowing what had happened to her, came and prostrated herself before him and told him the whole truth. And Jesus said to her, "Daughter, your trust has healed you. Go in peace, and be cured of your disease."

Before he had finished speaking, some

people came to the leader of the synagogue and said, "Your daughter is dead: why bother the rabbi any further?"

But Jesus overheard this, and said to him, "Don't be afraid; only trust." And he wouldn't let anyone go with him except Peter and James and John the brother of James.

And when they arrived at the leader's house, he found a great commotion, and loud sobbing and wailing. And he went in and said to them, "Why all this commotion? The child is not dead but sleeping." And they laughed at him.

But he ordered them all out, and took the child's father and mother and his three disciples, and went in to where the child was. And he took her hand and said, "*T'litha, koomi*" (which means, "Child, get up"). And immediately the girl got up and began to walk. And they were filled with great astonishment. And he told them to give her something to eat.

From there he went to Nazareth, his native town, and his disciples followed him.

And when the Sabbath came, he began to teach in the synagogue, and many people who heard him were bewildered, and said, "Where does this fellow get such stuff?" and "What makes *him* so wise?" and "How can he be a miracle-worker? Isn't this the carpenter, Mary's bastard, the brother of James and Joseph and Judas and Simon, and aren't his sisters here with us?" And they were prevented from believing in him.

And Jesus said, "A prophet is not rejected except in his own town and in his own family and in his own house."

And he was unable to do any miracle there, because of their disbelief.

8

And from there Jesus set out and went to the region around Tyre. And he went into a house, and didn't want anyone to know that he was there, but he couldn't remain hidden. For soon a Gentile woman, a Syrophoenician by race, heard of him, and came and prostrated

herself at his feet and said, "Take pity on me, sir; my daughter is possessed by a demon."

And he said to her, "It is not right to take the children's food and throw it to the dogs."

And she said, "True, sir; yet even the dogs under the table eat the children's scraps."

And Jesus answered, "Well said. Now go home; the demon has left your daughter."

And when she went home, she found the child lying in bed, and the derangement was gone.

And Jesus returned from the region of Tyre, and went by way of Sidon to the Sea of Galilee, through the region of the Decapolis.

And they brought him a man who was deaf and could hardly speak, and they begged him to lay his hands on him. And he took him aside, away from the crowd, and put his fingers into the man's ears, and spat and touched the man's tongue; and looking up into the sky, Jesus sighed, and said to him, "*Ethpatakh!*" (which means, "Be opened!") And immediately his ears were opened, his tongue was released, and he spoke clearly. And the people were exceedingly astonished.

And a woman in the crowd called out to him, "Blessed is the womb that bore you and the breasts that you sucked."

And Jesus said, "No: blessed rather are those who hear the word of God and obey it."

Another time, in Bethsaida, they brought a blind man to Jesus and begged him to touch him. And he took the blind man by the hand and led him out of the village; and he spat into his eyes, and laid his hands on them, and asked him, "Can you see anything?"

And he looked up and said, "I see men, like trees walking."

And Jesus again laid his hands on his eyes, and the man looked, and his sight was restored, and he could see everything distinctly.

Still another time, a man in the crowd said to him, "Rabbi, I brought you my son; he is pos-

sessed by a mute spirit, and when it attacks
him, it throws him around, and he foams and
grinds his teeth and gets stiff."

And they brought the boy to him; and
immediately he was thrown down violently,
and he thrashed around, foaming at the
mouth. And Jesus asked the father, "How
long has this been happening to him?"

And he said, "Since he was a child. It has
tried to kill him many times, and thrown him
into the fire or the water. But if it is possible
for you to do anything, take pity on us and
help us."

And Jesus said to him, "'*If* it is possible'!
Anything is possible when you believe it is."

And the boy's father cried out, "I believe;
help my unbelief."

And Jesus put his hands on the boy and
spoke to him. And the boy cried out and went
into convulsions, and then became like a
corpse, so that most of the people were saying
he had died. But Jesus took him by the hand
and lifted him, and he stood up.

Once, when they were in Capernaum, the disciples asked Jesus, "Who is the greatest in the kingdom of God?"

And he called a child over, and put him in front of them; and taking him in his arms, he said, "Truly I tell you, unless you return and become like children, you can't enter the kingdom of God."

Peter once asked him, "Sir, how often should I forgive my brother if he keeps wronging me? Up to seven times?"

And Jesus said to him, "Not just seven: seventy times seven."

9

Once a certain scribe stood up and said, "Rabbi, what must I do to gain eternal life?"

And Jesus said to him, "What is written in the Law?"

And the scribe said, "*You shall love the Lord your God with all your heart and with all your*

soul and with all your strength and with all your mind, and *You shall love your neighbor as yourself."*

And Jesus said, "You have answered correctly. Do this and you will live."

And the scribe said, "But who is my neighbor?"

And Jesus said, "A certain man, while traveling from Jerusalem to Jericho, was set upon by robbers, who stripped him and beat him and left him on the road, half dead. And a priest happened to be going down that road, and when he saw him, he passed by on the other side. And a Levite, too, came to that place and saw him and passed by on the other side. But a Samaritan who was traveling that way came upon the man, and when he saw him, he was moved with compassion, and he went over to him and bound up his wounds, pouring oil and wine on them, and put him on his own donkey and brought him to an inn and took care of him. And on the next day he took out two silver coins and gave them to the innkeeper and said, 'Take care of him; and if it costs more than this, I will reimburse you when I come back.'

"Which of these three, do you think, turned out to be a neighbor to that man?"

And the scribe said, "The one who treated him with mercy."

And Jesus said, "Go then, and do as he did."

Another time, the tax-gatherers and prostitutes were all crowding around to listen to him. And the scribes grumbled, and said, "This fellow welcomes criminals and eats with them."

And Jesus told them this parable. "What do you think: If a man has a hundred sheep and one of them strays, doesn't he leave the ninety-nine on the hills and go looking for the one that strayed? And when he finds it, he is filled with joy, and he puts it on his shoulders and goes home and gathers his friends and neighbors and says to them, 'Rejoice with me: I found my sheep that was lost.'

"Or if a woman has ten silver coins and

loses one of them, doesn't she light a lamp and sweep the house and keep searching until she finds it? And when she finds it, she gathers her friends and neighbors and says, 'Rejoice with me: I found the coin that I lost.' In just the same way, I tell you, God rejoices over one sinner who returns."

And he said, "There once was a man who had two sons. And the younger one said to him, 'Father, let me have my share of the estate.' So he divided his property between them. And not many days afterward, having turned his share into money, the younger son left and traveled to a distant country, and there he squandered his inheritance in riotous living. And after he had spent it all, a severe famine arose in that country; and he was destitute. And he went and hired himself out to a citizen of that country, who sent him to his farm to feed the pigs. And he longed to fill his belly with the husks that the pigs were eating; and no one would give him any food. And when he came to himself, he said, 'How many of my father's hired men have more than enough to eat, while I am dying of hunger. I will get up and go to my father, and say to him, "Father, I have sinned against God and against you, and I am no longer worthy to be called your son. Let me be like one of your hired men.'" And he got up, and went to his father. And while he was still a long way off, his father saw him, and was moved with compassion, and ran to him, and threw his arms around him, and kissed him. And the son said to him, 'Father, I have sinned against God and against you, and I am no longer worthy to be called your son.' But the father said to his servants, 'Quick, bring out the best robe we have and put it on him; and put a ring on his hand, and sandals on his feet. And bring the fatted calf, and kill it; and let us eat and make merry. For this son of mine was dead, and he has come back to life; he was lost, and is found.' And they began to make merry.

"Now the older son had been out in the

fields; and on his way home, as he got closer to the house, he heard music and dancing, and he called over one of the servants and asked what was happening. And the servant said, 'Your brother has come, and your father has killed the fatted calf, because he has him back safe and sound.' And he was angry and would not go in. And his father came out and tried to soothe him; but he said, 'Look: all these years I have been serving you, and never have I disobeyed your command. Yet you never even gave me a goat, so that I could feast and make merry with my friends. But now that this son of yours comes back, after eating up your money on whores, you kill the fatted calf for him!' And the father said to him, 'Child, you are always with me, and everything I have is yours. But it was proper to make merry and rejoice, for your brother was dead, and he has come back to life; he was lost, and is found.'"

10

And when Jesus had finished saying these things, he left Galilee and entered the territory of Judea. And large crowds gathered around him, and he healed and taught.

And some people were bringing children to him, for him to bless; but the disciples rebuked them. And when Jesus saw this, he was indignant, and said to them, "Let the children come to me, don't try to stop them; for the kingdom of God belongs to such as these. Truly I tell you, whoever doesn't accept the kingdom of God like a child cannot enter it." And he took them in his arms, and put his hands on them, and blessed them.

And one day, as he was setting out, a man ran up and fell on his knees before him, and said, "Good Rabbi, what must I do to gain eternal life?"

And Jesus said to him, "Why do you call

me good? No one is good except God alone. You know the commandments: *Do not murder, Do not commit adultery, Do not steal, Do not bear false witness, Do not defraud, Honor your father and mother.*"

And the man said, "Rabbi, all these I have kept since I was a boy."

And Jesus, looking at him, loved him, and said, "There is one thing that you lack: go, sell everything you have and give it to the poor, and you will have treasure in heaven; then come and follow me."

But when he heard this, his face clouded over, and he went away sick at heart, for he was a man who had large estates.

And Jesus looked around at his disciples and said, "Children, how hard it is for the rich to enter the kingdom of God. It is easier for a camel to go through the eye of a needle than for a rich man to enter the kingdom of God."

And as they were traveling along the road, he said to a certain man, "Follow me."

And the man said, "Let me first go and bury my father."

But Jesus said to him, "Let the dead bury their dead."

Another man said to Jesus, "I will follow you, sir, but let me first say good-bye to my family."

And Jesus said to him, "No one who puts his hand to the plow and then looks back is ready for the kingdom of God."

11

And as they came near Jerusalem, to Bethany and Bethphage and the Mount of Olives, the large crowds coming for the festival spread their cloaks in front of him on the road, and some people spread brushwood that they had cut in the fields. And those who walked in front of him and those who followed shouted, "Blessed is he who comes in the name of the Lord; praise God in the highest heavens!"

And when he entered Jerusalem, the whole city was stirred up, wondering who he was.

And the crowds said, "This is the prophet Jesus, from Nazareth in Galilee."

And he entered the Temple and looked around at everything; but since it was already late, he went out to Bethany with the Twelve.

And every day Jesus would go to the Temple to teach, and at night he would stay on the Mount of Olives. And early in the morning he would go back into the Temple, and all the people gathered around him, and he sat and taught them. And they listened to him with delight.

One day, as he was teaching in the Temple, some scribes said to him, "Rabbi, is it lawful to pay the tax to Caesar, or not?"

And Jesus said, "Bring me a coin."

And they brought one. And he said, "Whose image is on it?"

And they said, "Caesar's."

And Jesus said, "Give to Caesar the things that are Caesar's, and to God the things that are God's."

Later, a certain scribe who had been listening to Jesus and had observed how well he answered people's questions asked him, "Which commandment is the greatest of all?"

And Jesus answered, "*Hear, O Israel: the Lord our God is one; and you shall love the Lord your God with all your heart and with all your soul and with all your mind and with all your strength.* This is the first and greatest commandment. And there is a second one that is like it: *You shall love your neighbor as yourself.* On these two commandments all the Law and the prophets depend."

And the scribe said to him, "Excellent, Rabbi! You have said the truth, that God is one and there is no other beside him, and to love him with all your heart and all your understanding and all your strength, and to love your neighbor as yourself, is worth far more than all burnt offerings and sacrifices."

And Jesus, seeing that he had spoken wisely, said to him, "You are not far from the kingdom of God."

1 2

The next morning, as Jesus was teaching in the Temple, the scribes brought a woman who had been caught in adultery, and they stood her in the middle. And they said to him, "Rabbi, this woman was caught in adultery, in the very act. Moses in the Law commanded us to stone such women to death; what do *you* say?"

But Jesus stooped down and with his finger wrote on the ground.

And as they continued to question him, he stood up and said to them, "Let whoever of you is sinless be the first to throw a stone at her." And again he stooped down and wrote on the ground.

And when they heard this, they went out one by one, the older ones first. And Jesus was left alone, with the woman still standing there.

And Jesus stood up, and said to her,

"Woman, where are they? Has no one condemned you?"

And she said, "No one, sir."

And Jesus said, "I don't condemn you
either. Go now, and sin no more."

13

And the day before the Passover and the festival of Unleavened Bread, in the evening, he
came into the city with the Twelve, and they
ate supper. And after they had sung a psalm,
they went out to the Mount of Olives, across
the Kidron valley, to a garden called
Gethsemane.

And Jesus said, "Sit here, while I pray."
And going off by himself, he prostrated himself on the ground and prayed. And he said,
"Abba, all things are possible for you. Take
this cup from me. Nevertheless, not what I
want, but what you want."

And when he got up from his prayer and
went to the disciples, he found them asleep.

And he said to them, "Why are you sleeping? Couldn't you stay awake for even one hour?" And they didn't know what to answer.

And suddenly Judas came, one of the Twelve, with a battalion of Roman soldiers and some officers from the chief priests, carrying swords and clubs and lanterns and torches. And he went up to Jesus and said, "Rabbi!" and kissed him. And they seized Jesus and bound him, and took him away.

And all the disciples abandoned him, and fled.

14

And they took Jesus to the High Priest.

And Peter followed at a distance, into the courtyard of the High Priest. And the slaves and attendants had made a charcoal fire, because it was a cold night; and they were standing around the fire, warming themselves.

And Peter stood with them and warmed himself.

And one of the slave-girls of the High Priest came. And when she saw Peter, she looked at him closely and said, "You were there too, with that fellow from Nazareth, that Jesus." But he denied it, saying, "I don't know what you're talking about."

And after a while, someone else said to Peter, "You have a Galilean accent; you must be one of them." And he said, "God curse me if I know the man!" And at that moment the cock crowed. And Peter went out and burst into tears.

And early the next morning, the chief priests, with the elders and scribes, bound Jesus and took him away and handed him over to Pilate. And Pilate sentenced Jesus to death, and flogged him, and handed him over to his soldiers to be crucified.

And they took him out to crucify him, and seized a man named Simon of Cyrene, who

was passing by on his way in from the country, and made him carry the cross.

And they brought him to the place called Golgotha (which means "the place of the skull"). And some women offered him drugged wine, but he wouldn't take it.

And at about nine o'clock they crucified him.

And above his head the charge against him was written: THE KING OF THE JEWS. And with him they crucified two Zealots, one on his right and one on his left.

And at about three o'clock in the afternoon, Jesus uttered a loud cry, and died.